Upon This Rock,
I Will Build My Church

Reverend Gregory L. Williamson

ASA PUBLISHING CORPORATION
AN INNOVATIVE OUTSOURCE BOOK PUBLISHING HYBRID

ASA Publishing Corporation
1285 N. Telegraph Rd., PMB #351, Monroe, Michigan 48162
An Accredited Publishing House with the BBB

www.asapublishingcorporation.com

Copyrights©2024, Gregory L Williamson, All Rights Reserved
Book Title: Upon This Rock, I Will Build My Church
Date Published: 11.28.2024
Book ID: ASAPCID2380937
Edition: 1 *Trade Paperback*
ISBN: 978-1-960104-68-7
Library of Congress Cataloging-in-Publication Data

This book was published in the United States of America.
Great State of Michigan

Table of Contents

Forward i

Acknowledgments 1

Introduction... 5

Chapter 1

    Organizing the Church 19

        Footnotes 1A-1B.................................. 30

Chapter 2

    The Rock 43

        Footnotes 2A-2E.................................. 54

Chapter 3

    The Church's Purpose *and* Intent 59

        Footnotes 3A-3C.................................. 70

Chapter 4

    Obstacles *and* Challenges 73

        Footnotes 4A-4D.................................. 83

Chapter 5

    Church Finances *and* Budgeting 89

        Footnotes 5A-5E.................................. 103

Chapter 6

    The Church Family 107

        Footnotes 6A-6H.................................. 119

Chapter 7

    Education & Training 123

       Footnotes 7A-7G 134

Chapter 8

    Social *and* Political Responsibilities 139

       Footnotes 8A-8E 155

Chapter 9

    Summary 171

       Footnotes 9A-9G 196

Contributing Sources 203

Books by the Author
Reverend Gregory L. Williamson

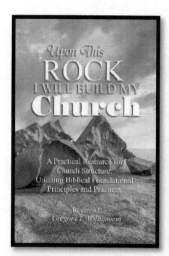
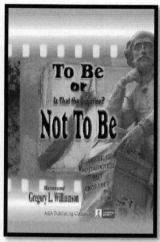

Purchases can be made from
Amazon | Barnes & Noble | Online Booksellers
Or through the Author, Reverend Gregory L. Williamson at
P.O. Box 555, Sale Creek, TN 37373 | Email: niamcso@gmail.com

A Forward by
Ray Glandon

I have known Reverend Gregory L. Williamson for years. I have edited magazines and books, and I would be hard-pressed to name anyone more knowledgeable, insightful, and capable of writing such an informative and instructional book.

His 40 plus years of ministerial experience provided him with valuable contacts, mentors, and fellow associates throughout this country. This accounts for his ability to honestly and succinctly explain the role of the church and its integral makeup.

This is an easy-to-read, very interesting and informative book that is not only for the layman but also a must for those in ministry who are seeking step-by-step guidance from a leader and expert in the field.

Acknowledgments

With each writing endeavor, there are so many late nights spent researching, reading, thinking, and of course, writing. Equally sacrificed is so much quality time that could be, and perhaps should be spent with family. I want to thank my wife, Janice, for all of the hours sacrificed during this project.

I am so thankful for my editor "Ray Glandon." He has consistently provided encouragement and motivation while elevating my writing to a grammatical level that far exceeds my ability. With each progressive book, he has demonstrated an ability to understand, often times, better than I do, what I'm trying to convey. You have been a blessing from God.

I'm grateful for the foundational support provided by my publisher, Steven Lawrence Hill, Sr., and the ASA Publishing team. Collectively, their experience and creativity continue to exceed my expectations.

Lastly, I acknowledge an extensive list of friends and great men and women of God who motivated me to take on this challenge. Their contributions have been invaluable. I have listed them alphabetically.

Pastor Billie D. Allen, Liberty Baptist, Dr. Robert E. Bailey, Trinity Baptist, Min. Morris Beaty, Mt. Canaan,

Pastor William Bell Jr., Genesis Christian, Dr. E. L. Branch, Third New Hope, Pastor James A Burr, Pastor James E. Burr, Pastor Eric Burr, Second New Hope, Pastor Will Cain, Elder Jerry Carson, Chaplaincy, Pastor Haman Cross, Jr., Rosedale Park, Pastor Dennis Culbreth, TBMB, Pastors Walter and Gail Davis, Saints Tabernacle, Antioch, and Evangel, The Late Samuel M. Edwards, Liberty Baptist, Dr. Tony Evans, Oak Cliff Bible, Pastor Micah Fries, Pastor Jake Gaines, Synagogue, The Late Dr. Claude Goodwin, Providence, Rev. William Harper, Rev Michael Harris, Pastor Gus Hernandez, Silverdale, The Late Dr. F. O. Hockenhull, First Trinity, Dr. Everett Jennings, New Providence, Rev. Eugene Jones, Liberty Baptist, Dr. Ternae Jordan, Sr., Mt Canaan, Pastor Gabriel Lewis, Dr. John MacArthur, Grace Community, Dr. Willie McLaurin, TBMB, Pastor James Minnick, Mt. Pleasant, Dr. Miles Monroe, Bahamas Faith Ministries International, Bishop Paul S. Morton, Changing A Generation Full Gospel, Pastor Anthony Payton, Come As You Are, Pastor Anthony Pettus Sr., Greater Progressive, Rev. James Pittman, Liberty Baptist, Rev. Tracy Pollard, Pastor Bill Robinson, South Park, Pastor Bruce Rogers, Jackson, TN, Rev. David Simmons, Elder Herb Taylor, Chaplaincy, Bishop Crystal B. Thomas, New Zion, Pastor Charles Thompson, Bible Fellowship, Rev. Lee A. Turner, Bishop Joseph W. Walker III, Mt. Zion, Pastor Wilbert Whatley, Rev. John Williams, Dean Pastor S. J. Williams, Third Baptist, Rev. Gary L. Williamson, Pastor Jessie Williamson,

Jackson, TN, Pastor Vincent Wolf, Oakdale Tabernacle.

This lofty list of men and women of God are pioneers who have inserted a salient stone in my moral and foundational understanding of church structure. Phenomenally, they have impacted my thoughts, beliefs, and knowledge of how the church can constructively navigate the Body of Christ from a holistic perspective. Those collective skills included practical techniques for preaching and teaching, the development of leadership skills, how to walk and operate in boldness and humility, and how to maintain firmness within the confines of compassion. Moreover, they emphasized the importance of demonstrating character, integrity, empathy, brotherly love, and tough love, all while remaining aware that the people we're leading and developing belong to God, not us.

Every principle I believe and hold, as it relates to church structure, has in some way been established by the truths I understand from God's word and the mentoring I have received from these men and women. The basic premise of our journey is very similar: develop within them a love for God, and a love for their fellow brothers and sisters.

Secondly, teach them to go throughout the world and make disciples by teaching His commandments. As we utilize those principles and practices detailed in scripture, God orchestrates relationships for our specific growth and development designed for us to complete our assignment. Most church leaders will not experience the magnitude of experienced, and successful church leaders who will mentor and share their best practices with them. I've had that experience, and I want to share their advice with others. I pray that the reader will benefit from those successes as well.

While my experiences may not reflect yours, I believe the applications will help you discover an appropriate solution in managing them. To assist in that endeavor, I have included various practical approaches to problem-solving in footnote sections after each chapter. These nuggets have been a God-Compass that has always pointed me north. I believe they will do the same for you.

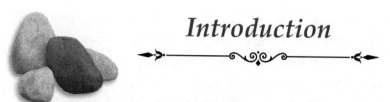

Introduction

Several books have been written on Church structure. Many of them focus on either mega-churches, or existing churches. For over 40 years, I've assisted in developing church leadership, administration, and ministry. I've witnessed too many new start-ups, new church plants, and a host of small congregations struggling unnecessarily in establishing a stable church structure. Too often, it has led to a delay in growth, and in some instances, to their demise.

When Jesus said to Peter, "Upon This Rock, I Will Build My Church," His focus was not on bricks, blocks, and mortar. He was not focusing on siding, pews, and sound systems; He was not conscripting schemes, gimmicks, or a charisma that would attract people. He was emphasizing a system: a system that focused on Him, in every aspect of the church structure. In Genesis, God completed His creation from a systematic approach. God also introduced a systematic approach to church structure. That process includes work, process, relationship, and commitment.

From this body of instruction, He points out that there are no shortcuts or alternative methods that will produce Godly character. It is only within the church structure that one will come to understand and acquire the fullness of being that is acceptable in God's eyes. If that's what you are seeking, this is the book for you. It provides a series of systematic processes and structures that find their support anchored in the scriptural teachings of Jesus. The anointed men and women He mentored during His earthly ministry are reflected in His teaching.

We are well aware that there are a variety of church types, what we refer to as denominational groups. Within those groups, various practices, approaches, and disciplines have been incorporated to give that particular group a unique differentiation within the Body of Christ. Ironically, those practices are essentially human, developed to give practical meaning to the beliefs and tenets held by that group. This book will focus on the foundational principles germane to all people's commitment to following the Messianic teachings of Jesus the Christ.

Throughout time, the Church has been viewed as a haven, a place of refuge, and a place of help in times of trouble and struggle. This is conceptually or theoretically truer in the African American church than it may be in others. During slavery, coming out of slavery, and even today, the church has been a bedrock in terms of support, advancement, education, and financial backing. At the same time, it has provided social, psychological, moral, and spiritual development. It is from that perspective that this book will offer a treasure of guidance.

If you are not part of an "African American"

church, let me remind you that there is only ONE church, and that church is the Church of God. Secondly, our God created us to be in relationship with Him and other believers in Christ. That begins now, not in heaven. There will be no division by denomination, race, or culture when we are raptured and united with our Lord. The learning and growth begin here, and the sooner we understand that and go after it, the sooner the unity of the spirit development can begin.

Make every effort to preserve the unity the Spirit has already created, with peace binding you together.

Ephesians 4:3

So, as I mentioned earlier, Jesus, the great unifier, introduced a system to His disciples. Within this system, the church is to be built. The church is not the buildings we construct. It's the disciples we make, mentor, and develop to conduct services within them. Jesus understood that man is a spiritual being, but He also understood that there were and are many other developmental needs that man needs to be complete. Jesus also fully understood that Satan would be actively engaged in a full-blown effort to impede that process. Nevertheless, He assured Peter, and He assures us that *"The Rock,"* *upon which He builds His church*, reigns victorious, despite Satan's futile attempts to destroy it.

Why was He so sure of that, and why are we to be equally certain of the same? It's because "The Rock" upon which the church is built is Jesus Himself. It is the application of Jesus and His teachings to our every challenging encounter in life that this book will illustrate, explain, and provide direction.

This is why I have called you Peter (rock): for on this rock I will build My church. The church will reign triumphant even against the gates of hell.

Matthew 16:18

The Super Bowl is one of the most watched sports events across the country, perhaps even the world. Those who may not be sports advocates are still somehow drawn into the final game of the season that determines the NFL champion. The halftime show, *depending on the performers*, can often create great interest as well.

The New England Patriots may not be your favorite team, but many believe that during the Tom Brady era, it may have been one of the best football organizations in NFL history. However, some may argue that the New England Patriots were not the elite of the NFL, and Tom Brady isn't the (GOAT) *greatest of all time*. I just want to use them to support a point. It's difficult to disagree that they may have created the most refined football system of all time. It is from that perspective that I want to explore the purpose and intent of the church and how it relates to the "rock" that Jesus referenced in Matthew 16:18.

Systems, if utilized properly and efficiently, can prove to be most effective. Allow me to use the NBA to make another point, relative to systems. In 2004, the Detroit Pistons met the Los Angeles Lakers in the NBA championship series. Most analysts wrote off the Pistons as having no chance to win that series. The reason was obvious: The Lakers, through development, trades, and recruitment had some of the best players in their position.

They intended to create an unstoppable team by acquiring what many believed were the best players at every position. Statistically, they may have accomplished their objective. What they later discovered, however, was that the best players still need a corporate strategy or team system to be effective and efficient.

On paper, Ben Wallace, Rasheed Wallace, Chauncey Billups, Richard Hamilton, and Tashaun Prince were no match for Shaquille O'Neil, Kobe Bryant, Rick Fox, Karl Malone, and Gary Payton. What the Lakers didn't realize was that the Pistons had a system, and everyone knew their role and operated within it. If you recall that series, you know that the Pistons beat the Lakers in 5 games. Some fans thought, except for some of the calls from the referees, the Lakers would have been swept in four games. Whether it was four or five games, the Pistons came out with the victory.

Well, God designed the church as a system too, and it is most effective and efficient when it operates that way. When the church (The Body of Believers) discovers its unique role, accepts it, and operates within it, its potential is unlimited, and its impact is efficient and undeniable. It may not be what we think it should look like, but it will certainly be what God has designed it to be.

Other than a couple of references in Numbers and Ecclesiastes, there is no direct mention of the word, "church" in the Old Testament. There are references inferred if we look at words, such as assembly, congregation, house of God, and other similar nouns. However, a clear and decisive use of the word, "church" is not recorded. It's not until we reach the New Testament that we find the establishment of the church. We find the first reference in the passage in Matthew 16:18.

In this passage, Jesus says to Peter, "Upon this rock, I will build my church." Jesus used the Greek word "ekklesia" when He referenced the church. Ekklesia means an assembly or gathering of people. *The church is much like an embassy. The U.S. has embassies throughout the world, and the people working at an embassy are expected to live out the values of the laws of the United States, as they* represent their homeland in a foreign country. Each embassy then is viewed as a microcosm of America, but yet a far distance away from America.

The church, in a similar way, is a system that God designed to operate on the principles of our Lord Jesus Christ, and it should operate or adopt the agenda of its heavenly King and enact those principles on Earth. More simply put, the church is a microcosm of heaven, albeit a long way from it, but designed to withstand the authority of hell's attempts to destroy it. When the system of God's given authority is executed, hell's attempt to impede the church's progress is foiled.

When Jesus says to Peter, "Upon this rock, I will build my church," we must remember that just before this statement, the disciples were asked, "Who do people say that the Son of Man is?" Peter spoke for the group and said, "You are the Christ." Jesus acknowledged Peter's response as a revelation from God, but He addressed Peter using the Greek form and meaning of his name, "Petros," which means stone. When Jesus said, "Upon this rock, I will build My church," He used the Greek word "Petra," which means a collection of rocks, knitted together to form a larger slab. Thus, Jesus's church would be comprised of His unified followers who would confess Him as the Christ, the Son of the living God, just as Peter did.

There are people today who believe Jesus was saying to Peter, "I will build my church upon you (Peter)." That is bad theology. Nowhere else in scripture do we find any reference to the church being founded upon Peter. On the contrary, there are countless examples of Jesus being the cornerstone and very foundation of the church. This is just one example of how division creeps into the body of Christ. It also speaks to the riff and discord in relationships and apologetics among varying believers. How blessed are we that the church is founded on Jesus Christ, a perfect foundation, and not on Peter, a flawed and fallible one!

So, what is the meaning of the pronouncement that Jesus made? A brief synopsis might suggest that Jesus was telling Peter and the other disciples that this collection of "rocks," knitted together to form the larger slab would be much like Paul's words in *I Corinthians 12*. Paul says -

The Spirit is not just an impersonal force or feeling; He is just as much a person within the Trinity as the Father and the Son. Accordingly, the Spirit chooses where to impart gifts, as He works together with the Father and Son, to build up the church.

That's the perspective to build on. A collection of rocks that form a more effective and functional slab is what the church was meant to be. Jesus demonstrated this during His earthly ministry. He didn't go about randomly quoting scripture, setting up fund-raisers, or establishing annual days like usher's anniversaries or Men's Day services. Jesus utilized people and opportunities to make a difference in their lives. He accomplished that by building people up, restoring their integrity, and healing the obstacles that impeded their ability to live constructive and productive lives. The church can effectively do the same today, but it will require a different approach.

God created man, and His purpose was, and is now, to have an intimate relationship with him. He wants man to see Him as the Almighty God (Jehovah Elohim) who loves him and desires to lead, guide, protect, and provide for him. Man complicates this process by trying to navigate his own life and creating for himself other lesser gods. Therein is the beginning of the problems we see on vast display throughout our land. The good news is that this problem can be corrected. Sin and mankind's sinful nature are what brought us to where we are. God, however, provided a cure for this condition when He sacrificed His only begotten Son as a ransom and propitiation for our nature. We have been allowed to correct our relationship with Him by accepting the atoning sacrifice of His Son.

God expressed His love for the world in this way: He gave His only Son so that whoever believes in Him will not face everlasting destruction, but will have everlasting life.

John 3:16

Accepting the atoning sacrifice of Jesus Christ is just the beginning phase of inclusion into the Body of

Christ (the Church). Finding contentment there perpetuates the current state of affairs in too many churches. The majority of its members are comfortably content with sitting in pews each week, while a minority of members are slowly and methodically wearing themselves out.

All churches belong to God, and consequently, all church members belong to Him as well. Church members (the Church) are the collective "rocks" that Jesus says create the larger slab when knitted together. God's commitment to protect the church from the destructive attacks of Satan is trustworthy, reliable, and consistent with His character. What that larger slab looks like weighs heavily on the church's willingness to follow God's divine plan.

The Old Testament confirms as it relates to the church, that its eminent purpose was given to particular persons who God declared were faithful and holy. Abraham and David are two individuals who acquired that distinction in the Old Testament. In the New Testament, Jesus ascribes this agency to Peter, but He does not in any way give him supreme authority over the church, or any of his successors. The church is Christ's peculiar people, and they belong to him. *The world is God's, and they that dwell therein;* but the church is a chosen remnant that stands in relationship with God through Christ as our Mediator. The church displays His image and likeness. Psalm 24:1 reminds us of this fact.

The church is comprised of several believing men and women. They are called out of the world, set apart from it, and therefore dedicated to the cause of Christ. It is not *our* church, it belongs to God. Peter conveys this truth in I Peter 5:2-4 when he admonished ministers to –

Feed the flock of God, not to lord it over God's people, and when the chief Shepherd shall appear, ye shall receive a crown of glory. The Builder and Maker of the church is Christ himself. The church is the temple of God and Christ is the Builder (Zech. 6:11-13 & I Corinthians 6:19). By the power of the Holy Spirit through the preaching of his word, He adds souls to His church, and so builds it up with living stones, (1 Pet. 2:4-5).

We are God's building, and the building process is a progressive work. The foundation on which it is built is *this Rock.* It is incumbent upon us to let the architect do his part in developing the church by developing us.

The church is built upon a rock: *a firm, strong, and lasting foundation,* which time will not waste, and it will not sink under the weight of the building. Christ would not build his house upon the sand, for he knew that storms would arise. *A rock is high,* (Ps. 61:2). Christ's church does not stand upon a level with this world; *a rock is large,* and extends far, as does the church's foundation. The larger and greater the rock, the stronger the foundation.

In conjunction with the concept of the church, or Body of Christ, being the rocks that God uses to build His church, the principles upon which Jesus taught and utilized during His earthly ministry are also rocks and pillars. As rocks and pillars of God's purpose, we must remember that God's word is reliable and dependable. Whether Old or New Testament, His word is infallible.

We rest in this hope we've been given—the hope that we will live forever with our God—the hope that He proclaimed ages and ages ago (even before time began). And our God is no liar; He is not even capable of uttering lies.

Titus 1:2

God's Word applies to every aspect of our life, including all aspects of church structure. II Timothy 3:16 says –

All Scripture is God-breathed and given by divine inspiration, and is profitable for instruction, for conviction of sin, for correction of error and restoration to obedience, for training in righteousness; learning to live in conformity to God's will, both publicly and privately in behaving honorably with personal integrity and moral courage.

Therefore, the credibility of the postulations of this

work is predicated on the reader's acceptance of God's Word being the Sovereign authority of what is right and true. That is applicable as it relates to the best practices when setting up or applying appropriate principles to church structure and what it encompasses. Now that the premise has been established and the foundation has been laid, I submit that the church is the one entity that can and should provide clear and concise direction for growth and maturity in the Body of Christ.

While salvation absolves mankind's greatest problem; *his sin problem*, man's needs are more extensive and substantial than salvation alone. Abraham Maslow was an American psychologist. He is best known for *Maslow's* hierarchy of needs, a theory of psychological health, predicated on fulfilling innate human needs in priority, culminating in self-actualization. He was not a theologian, thus he did not focus specifically on man's spiritual needs. However, mankind's physical, psychological, emotional, social, educational, and financial health are equally essential in the development of his overall well-being and completeness.

This book will collectively delve into those areas with the inclusive intent of addressing church structure from a holistic perspective.

Chapter 1
Organizing the Church

Here are my instructions: diligently guard yourselves, and diligently guard the whole flock over which the Holy Spirit has given you oversight. Shepherd the church of God, this precious church which He made His own, through the blood of His own Son.

Acts 20:28

Luke explains in great detail the level of importance and significance that God places on His church. He also reminds us that it was the precious blood of Jesus that was shed for it. Every decision made and position taken should be filtered through those instructions. Every church organization will be somewhat different because its leadership and body have differing personalities and assignments. The methodology of ministry will differ from church to church, but the message should and must remain constant.

Every church has an assignment, based on its calling and purpose. The call is usually communicated and presented by one or more given the unction to organize. The responsibility of organizing a church usually comes about for one or two purposes: either a minister or a group of believers have been called to establish a new church group (Body of Believers) or, an existing church is in need of organizational structure. Either way, enormous effort must go into this undertaking proactively if prodigious results are to be expected.

Most organizers of any project believe the initiation of organizing is much easier with a new beginning than it is when choreographing a change in an existing structure. I agree with this position, but it should be understood that new start-ups also have their own set of challenges to manage. Whether it's a new church plant or an existing church, organizing must begin with petitioning God for direction. Those prayers must be corporate, fervent, and beseeched from a dedicated body of committed believers. Only God can effectively prepare a church for its beginning and its future: at the beginning. **See Footnote 1A, Page 30-36**

My thoughts and My ways are above and beyond you, just as heaven is far from your reach here on earth.

Isaiah 55:9

Proper planning during the organizing process does not mean that the church won't encounter problems, challenges, and issues. The Church is composed of God's called out body of believers and because Satan knows this, he places a target on the Church. With that in mind, improper planning, or the failure to plan, opens the church to severe opposition.

Problems, challenges, issues, and struggles are to be expected in "Church Business" because the church encompasses people from all walks of life, and many times, at their worst. We must remember, when God is the organizer, you have the greatest resource at your disposal. It may get rough, but He will guide you along the way.

Planning and organizing a church without consulting God is a perfect recipe for difficulties, but not failure. The Body of Christ must stay cognizant of the fact that God assures us,

No weapon that is formed against thee shall prosper; and every tongue that shall rise against thee in judgment thou shalt condemn. This is the heritage of the servants of the LORD, and their righteousness is of me, saith the LORD.

Isaiah 54:17

These words are reliable because,

The weapons of our warfare are not carnal, but mighty through God to the pulling down of strong holds;

II Corinthians 10:4

Prepare, arrange, structure, coordinate, and delegate; these are all verbs that define the organizational process. Every organizational effort should have these qualities at its core if its expected outcome is success. Equally true is the fact that one person (*unless that one person is Jesus Christ Himself*) cannot successfully accomplish this task alone. Thus, when the organizational process begins, it will require a group effort. As it relates to the organizing of the church, all preparation, arrangements, structure, coordination, and delegation must include and involve the doctrines, beliefs, principles, and precepts of the teachings of God. Its demonstration should reflect what was modeled by Jesus Christ. It should be empowered by the Holy Spirit.

One man or woman may be called to organize a church, but the underpinnings of its structure will be contingent upon a group effort. When God gives an assignment of that magnitude and intensity, it is to address a need that extends beyond the individual called to carry out the assignment. The leader or facilitator is just that: the person God has chosen to initiate the mission, but continuous others will provide assistance in completing the objective. One example of this process is Moses. Although one of the greatest leaders God has ever developed and utilized, he was instructed to use other individuals to carry out his assignment. At Numbers 1:1-5 and 16-19, we find these instructions -

The LORD spoke to Moses in the tent of meeting in the Wilderness of Sinai, on the first day of the second

month of the second year after Israel's departure from the land of Egypt: Take a census of the entire Israelite community by their tribes and their ancestral houses, counting the names of every male one by one. You and Aaron are to register those who are 20 years old or more by their military divisions—everyone who can serve in Israel's army. A man from each tribe is to be with you, each one the head of his ancestral house. These men will assist you.

These are the men called from the community; they are leaders of their ancestral tribes, the heads of Israel's families. So, Moses and Aaron took these men who had been designated by name, and they assembled the whole community on the first day of the second month. They recorded their ancestry by their clans and their ancestral houses, counting one by one the names of those 20 years old or more, just as the Lord commanded Moses. He registered them in the Wilderness of Sinai:

Moses was no less of a leader by following these instructions. He was not deficient of the necessary leadership skills required to complete the assignment. He was simply and obediently utilizing the people God gave him to get the job done. That's what God does. He gives an assignment, provides the resources, and infuses the leader with the instructions to make it happen.

Good leaders are those who can delegate tasks and

make sure that everyone on their team is learning, growing, and being challenged. When leaders do the work that should be assigned to their colleagues, they end up hurting themselves. They become stressed out because they are overloaded with the work. Their colleagues get confused, stressed, or bored, and they may want to leave.

God provides the instructions for organizing His church through various means. Some of it will come through various practical applications, but most of it will come through the correct application of His word, in scripture. Organizers can benefit from the wise counsel of other organizers that have both failed and succeeded in prior endeavors. While no two churches will be identical in structure, they should be very similar in their foundational principles and practices.

Careful consideration must be given to the incorporation of other church practices. Structure varies from one church group to another because God has placed a unique set of gifted and talented individuals within that body to affect and inject specific needs germane to that calling. Improper assessment or simply duplicating what works with another church can, and often does negate the joy and pride of originality.

This is equally true with the roles and responsibilities assigned to administration personnel. Structural responsibilities can, and often will look very similar. The assigning of people to those responsibilities is where variation enters. Yes, God gives to all of us unique and powerful gifts. Yes, God gives to every church everything (people & resources) they need to complete the assignment. But no, that picture will not look the same in every church. **See Footnote 1B, Page 36-42**

The writer of Proverbs says this about wisdom –

A wise man will hear, and will increase learning; and a man of understanding shall attain unto wise counsels:

Proverbs 1:5

Hear counsel, and receive instruction, that thou may continue to be wise in thy latter end.

Proverbs 19:20

Even though people do their best, in making plans for their lives; it is God that guides their steps.

Proverbs 16:9

The apostle Paul supports that concept when he says to us –

All Scripture is inspired by God, and is profitable for teaching, for rebuking, for correcting, for training in righteousness, so that the man of God may be complete, equipped for every good work.

II Timothy 3:16

Organizing the church requires a two-fold perspective – Its administrative functionality and its spiritual objective. An example of God's administrative functionality can be seen in Exodus 18:17-22 where Moses's father-in-law said,

What you are doing is not good for you. The responsibility is just too much. You are going to wear yourself out. Not only that, you're going to wear out the people too. You can't do it all by yourself. I am going to give you a piece of advice, so listen up and God will be with you. You should represent the people before God, and carry their concerns to Him. Teach them God's requirements and pass on His laws. Show them the right way to live and the kind of work they should be doing. As for all these other duties you have taken on, choose competent leaders who fear God, love truth, despise dishonesty, and won't take bribes. After you divide and subdivide all the people into various groups of a thousand, hundred, fifty, and ten, put the men of integrity you selected in charge over the various groups. Let these righteous leaders be ready to judge the people whenever it is necessary. If there is some major problem, they can bring that to you. Otherwise, these select leaders ought to be able to handle the minor problems.

The spiritual objective is well communicated throughout the New Testament. Matthew 28:19-20, Jesus says –

All authority in heaven and on earth is given to me. So go and make followers of all people in the world. Baptize them in the name of the Father and the Son and the Holy Spirit. Teach them to obey everything that I have told you to do. You can be sure that I will be with you always. I will continue with you until the end of time.

The church in Judea, Galilee, and Samaria had a time of peace. And with the help of the Holy Spirit, these groups of believers became stronger in faith and showed their respect for the Lord by the way they lived. So the church grew in numbers all over.

Acts 9:31

So Peter was kept in jail, but the church was constantly praying to God for him.

Acts 12:5

In the church at Antioch there were some prophets and teachers. They were Barnabas, Simeon (also called Niger), Lucius (from the city of Cyrene), Manaen (who had grown up with King Herod), and Saul. So the church fasted and prayed. They laid their hands on Barnabas and Saul and sent them out.

Acts 13:1-3

The church helped them get ready to leave on their trip. The men went through the countries of Phoenicia and Samaria, where they told all about how the non-Jewish people had turned to the true God. This made all the believers extremely happy. When the men arrived in Jerusalem, the apostles, the elders, and the whole church welcomed them. Paul, Barnabas, and Silas told the others about everything God had done with them. Paul and Silas went through the countries of Syria and Cilicia, helping churches grow stronger. Churches were growing in their faith, and the number of believers was growing every day - Acts 15 & 16.

Within the church, God has given a place first to apostles, second to prophets, and third to teachers. Then God has given a place to those who do miracles, those who have gifts of healing, and those who can help others, those who are able to lead, and those who can speak in different kinds of languages.

I Corinthians 12:28

God put everything under Christ's power and made him head over everything for the church. The church is

Christ's body. It is filled with him. He makes everything complete in every way. His purpose was that all the rulers and powers in the heavenly places will now know the many different ways he shows his wisdom. They will know this because of the church.

Ephesians 1-3

These are just some of the many instructions we have as it relates to the administrative and spiritual aspects of church structure.

Be careful for yourselves and for all the people God has given you. The Holy Spirit gave you the work of caring for this flock. You must be shepherds to the church of God, the people he bought with his own blood.

Acts 15:3-4

Footnotes - 1A-1B

Footnote 1A – Church Leadership and Methodology

There are many leadership styles. Each leadership style has a purpose and is effective when properly positioned. Matching the most effective leadership style with a particular church body is critical to its success. A list of leadership styles are provided below.

Autocratic Leadership

It's centered on the boss. The leader holds all authority and responsibility. Leaders make decisions on their own without consulting anyone else. They reach decisions, communicate them to others, and expect prompt implementation. The autocratic environment normally has little or no flexibility. Guidelines, procedures, and policies are all natural additions of an autocratic leader. There are very few situations that can actually support autocratic leadership as it is often damaging long-term.

Democratic Leadership

In this leadership style, others are involved in making decisions. Unlike autocratic, the headship is centered on the contribution of others. The democratic leader makes the final decision, but he or she is known to delegate authority to other people, who may suggest various projects. The most unique feature of this leadership is that communication is active upward and downward. Democratic leadership is one of the most preferred leadership styles, and it requires fairness, competence, creativity, courage, intelligence, and honesty.

Strategic Leadership

The strategic leader fills the gap between the need for new possibilities and the need for practicality by providing a strict set of behaviors. Effective strategic leadership usually delivers productive results in terms of what the church naturally expects from its leadership in times of change.

Transformational Leadership

This leadership style is all about initiating change in groups, oneself, and others. Statistically, transformational leadership tends to have more committed and satisfied followers. This is primarily because transformational leaders empower their followers.

Team Leadership

Team leadership involves the creation and projection of a vivid vision of its future, where it is heading and what it will stand for. The vision inspires and provides a strong sense of purpose and direction. Team leadership is about working with the hearts and minds of all those involved. The most challenging aspect of this leadership is whether or not it will succeed. According to Harvard Business Review, team leadership may fail because of poor leadership qualities.

Cross-Cultural Leadership

This form of leadership normally exists where there are various cultures in the church. Particularly, international churches require leaders who can effectively adjust their leadership to work across cultures.

Transactional Leadership

This leadership style maintains or continues the status quo. Transactional leadership can sound rather basic, with its focus on an exchange. Being clear, focusing on expectations, and giving feedback are all important leadership skills. Transactional leadership involves clarifying what is expected of its members and explaining to them how to meet those expectations.

Coaching Leadership

Coaching leadership requires teaching and supervising members. The Basic premise behind this style of leadership is to improve the skill-set of the members through coaching. Coaching leadership accomplishes this through motivation, inspiration, and encouragement.

Charismatic Leadership

In this leadership style, charismatic leaders demonstrate their innovative power. Charisma actually involves a transformation of the followers' values and beliefs. The intent of the charismatic leader is to transform the underlying normative proclivity that structures specific attitudes.

Visionary Leadership

This form of leadership involves leaders who recognize that the method and processes of leadership are all obtained with and through people. Most great and successful leaders have the aspects of vision in them. However, those who are highly visionary are the ones considered to be exhibiting visionary leadership. Outstanding leaders will always transform their visions into realities.

Pace-Setting Leadership

This leadership style describes a very driven leader who sets the pace, as in racing. Pacesetters set the bar high and push their team members to run hard and fast to the finish line. While this style is effective in getting things done, it's a style that can hurt team members. Even the most driven employees may become stressed working under this style of leadership. This is a short-term style. A pace-setting leader needs to let the air out of the tires once in a while to avoid causing team burnout. "Do as I do!"

Affiliative Style

The affiliative leadership approach is one where the leader gets up-close and personal with people. A leader practicing this style pays attention to and supports the emotional needs of team members. The leader strives to open up a pipeline that connects him or her to the team. This style is all about forming collaborative relationships with teams. It is useful in smoothing conflicts or reassuring people during times of stress. "People come first."

Laissez-Faire Style

This leadership style involves the least amount of oversight. On the surface, a laissez-faire leader may appear to trust people to know what to do. It is, however, beneficial to give people opportunities to spread their wings with a total lack of direction, people may unintentionally drift in the wrong direction— away from the critical goals of the organization. This style can work if you're leading highly skilled, experienced people who are self-starters and motivated. To be most effective with this style, it is necessary to monitor team performance and provide regular feedback.

Each leadership style has its benefits when used in the appropriate environment. When used independently, they might be looked at as "Do as I say," "Follow my Vision," "Follow Me," "Do as I do!," "People come first," "Consider this," or "What do you think?"

Knowing which of the leadership styles works best for you is part of being a good leader. Developing a signature style with the ability to utilize other styles as the situation warrants, may enhance your leadership effectiveness. Get familiar with the catalogue of leadership styles that can work best for a given situation. Ask yourself what skills you need to develop.

Start by raising your awareness of your dominant leadership style. You can do this by asking trusted colleagues to describe the strengths of your leadership style. You can also take a leadership style assessment. Be honest when assessing what approach you use. Moving from a dominant leadership style to a different one may be challenging, but practice the new attributes until they become natural. Don't use a different leadership style because someone else is having success with it. Always remember, authenticity will yield the greater results.

Traditional leadership styles may be relevant and effective in some churches today, but they may need to be combined with new approaches. Leading the 21st century church requires collective innovation. Today's church environments are loaded with unique challenges due to the changing demographics and the varying expectations of a diverse congregation. This may call for a new breed of leader who is able to fuse most of the leadership styles discussed here. Flexibility in adapting to other leadership styles may be the ultimate character trait necessary to lead today's multi-talented environment.

Note – For the sake of advancing the kingdom of God and maintaining integrity in the clergy arena, retaining a leader whose style is unable to provide a progressive movement is counterproductive. Making the necessary adjustment does not depict failure. However, failing to make a change will. I have sadly watched too many churches crash as age demographics significantly changed within the congregation, but the style of leadership to effectively reach them didn't.

Footnote 1B – *Preparation, arrangement, structure, coordination, and delegation.*

Every organizational effort should have these qualities at its core if its expected end is success. As it relates to the organizing of the church, all preparation, arrangements, structure, coordination, and delegation must include and involve the doctrines, beliefs, principles, and precepts of the teachings of God.

One man or woman may be called to organize a church, but the underpinnings of its structure will be contingent upon a group effort. When God gives an assignment of that magnitude and intensity, it is to address a need that extends beyond the individual called to carry out the assignment. The leader or facilitator is just that: the leader or person God has chosen to initiate the mission, but others will provide assistance in completing the objective.

The primary purpose for organizing or planting a church is to focus on saving the lost. Included in that function is teaching, developing, growing, and discipling them for mission work. The message is simple - *For the Son of man is come to seek and to save that which was lost (Luke 19:10). For God so loved the world, that he gave his only begotten Son, that whosoever believeth in him should not perish, but have everlasting life (John 3:16). But God proves his love toward us, in that, while we were yet sinners, Christ died for us (Romans 5:8). This is the message of faith that we proclaim: If you confess with your mouth, "Jesus is Lord," and believe in your heart that God raised Him from the dead, you will be saved (Romans 10:8-9). Go, therefore, and make disciples of all nations, baptizing them in the name of the Father and of the Son and of the Holy Spirit, teaching them to observe everything I have commanded you. And remember, I am with you always, to the end of the age (Matthew 28:19-20).*

These are just some of the basic purposes that every

church should be focused on. The method or how the church intends to accomplish these endeavors may vary. That is usually where you begin to see the personality, talents, and gifting of the leader and/or leadership group. This engagement should not be underestimated. Significant thought, prayer, and supplication must be priority. God has sanctioned the organizing of a church. He has a specific and unique purpose for each church, beyond the aforementioned purpose above. He has designated a leader to accomplish this purpose. He will provide both direction and resources to get there. A very important part of these resources is contained in the church planting group, and the people that God sends/directs to each church body.

Preparation: There needs to be an agreed upon mission statement for the church. The mission statement provides the focus, goal, and direction for the church body. Any practice that doesn't align with the mission statement should either be put aside or the mission statement should be amended to include it. Careful and considerable thought and prayer should be utilized in the planning of the mission statement. You do not want to be a church that constantly amends or changes its direction, nor do you want to be a church that does not model its mission.

Note - When preparing the church's mission statement,

the focus should reflect the unique calling that impacts the environmental needs of the community in which the church exists.

Arrangement: How the church is arranged should be based on biblical examples (clergy, deacons, trustees, administrators, etc.) and the available skill-set of the people God has provided. The arrangement of duties and responsibilities may change over time. As people with additional or more advanced abilities are added, adjustments may become necessary. You should always prepare and position the most suitable people in positions to grow and develop the church body. It should be made clear from the beginning that God is the only owner of the church, and every position held within it is a servant position.

By no means am I affirming that degrees, seniority, or prior experience should dictate who's placed into a position in the church. It could be a significant factor, but those qualities do not automatically indicate the most suitable fit.

*Note – Many years ago, a young man that grew up in a particular church went away to college. After graduating, he returned to the church with a degree in accounting. He expressed interest in utilizing his accounting knowledge to computerize the churches finances. His offer was met with great resistance. The church was comfortable with pen and paper records and did not trust computers, so they rejected

the offer. The truth of the matter was the financial record-keeper had been performing this job for almost two decades and did not want to be replaced by a computer.

Transitions must be carefully planned out. When they involve people, feelings quickly enter the picture. That didn't happen. As a result, the pen and paper trail continued. After several unsuccessful efforts, the young man eventually moved to another church where he was transitioned into their financial accounting position, where he continues to serve today. This was an occasion where the degree and experience warranted the position, but because the church did not have a transitional plan in place, they missed a great opportunity.

Structure: The illustration above is just one reason why structure is so important to the success and failure of many churches. Great opportunities come and go because the proper protocols have not been addressed and/or put in place. Structure is simply the arrangement and relationship between the parts or elements of something complex. The dynamics of a church warrant occasional re-arrangement to improve working relations because it is a complex organization.

Coordination: Generally, most churches begin with a basic or flat organizational structure.

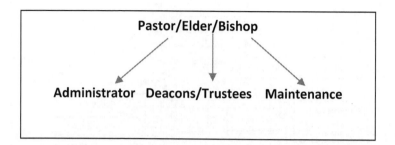

Pastor/Elder/Bishop

Administrator   Deacons/Trustees   Maintenance

However, as the church grows, programs expand, and missions and outreach increase, the need for greater coordination intensifies. Structure and coordination go hand in hand. The first task is to find the appropriate structure that fits and will best facilitate the objectives of the church. Even after its discovery, implementation involves a strategic process as well. Whether it's a new structure or a transition from an existing one, the process can be overwhelming. Compare the two charts.

Delegation: Perhaps every pastor gets excited when growth occurs, both in quality and quantity. Each dimension of growth requires significant changes to the infrastructure of the church. Growth is constructive, but consistent proactive planning, delegation, and organizing must become a common practice if success and sustainability are the desired outcome.

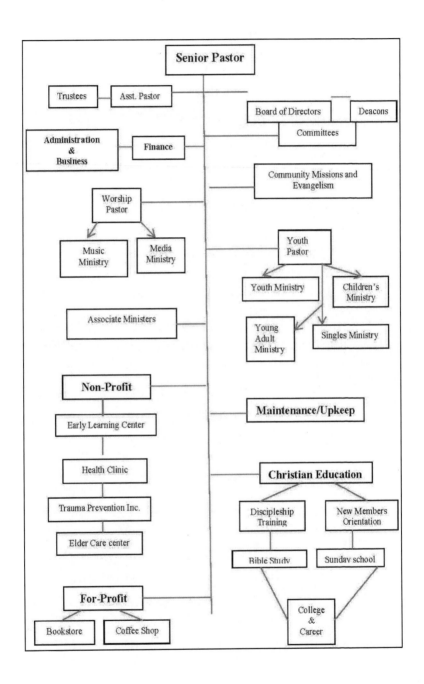

Chapter 2
The Rock

This is why I have called you, Peter (rock): for on this rock I will build My church. The church will reign triumphant even against the gates of hell.

Matthew 16:18

Other than a couple of references in Numbers and Ecclesiastes, there is no direct mention of the word "church" in the Old Testament. There are inferences if we consider words like assembly, congregation, house of God, and other similar citations, but a clear and decisive use of the word "church" is not recorded. It's not until the New Testament that we find the establishment of the church. That first reference is uttered by our Lord Jesus in the passage at Matthew 16:18.

In this passage, Jesus says to Peter, upon this rock, I will build my church. Jesus used the Greek word "ekklesia" when He referenced the church. Ekklesia is defined as an assembly or gathering of people. The church is much like an embassy. The U.S. has embassies throughout the world, and the people working at an embassy are expected to live out the values of the laws of the United States, as they represent their homeland in a foreign country. Each embassy then is viewed as a microcosm of America, but a far distance away from America. **See Footnote 2A, Page 54.**

The church, in a similar way, is a system that God designed to operate on the principles of our Lord Jesus Christ. It should not only operate or adopt the agenda of its heavenly King but also enact those principles on earth. More simply put, the church is a microcosm of heaven, albeit, a long way from it, designed to withstand the authority of hell's attempts to destroy it. When the system of God's given authority is executed, hell's attempt to impede the church's progress is foiled.

When Jesus says to Peter, "Upon this rock, I will build my church," you might recall that just before this statement, the disciples were asked, *"Who do people say that the Son of Man is?"* Peter spoke for the group and said, *"You are the Christ."* Jesus acknowledged Peter's response as a revelation from God, but He addressed Peter using the Greek form and meaning of his name, "Petros," which means stone. However, when Jesus said, "Upon this rock, I will build My church," Jesus used the Greek word "Petra," which means a collection of rocks knitted together to form a larger slab. Thus, Jesus's church would be comprised of His unified followers who would confess Him as the Christ, the Son of the living God, just as Peter did. **See Footnote 2B, Page 55.**

There are people today who believe Jesus was saying to Peter, I will build my church upon you (Peter). That is bad theology. Nowhere else in scripture do we find any reference to the church being founded upon Peter. On the contrary, there are countless examples of Jesus being the cornerstone and very foundation of the church. This is just one example of how division creeps into the body of Christ. It also speaks to the riff and discord in relationships and apologetics among varying believers. How blessed we are in that the church is founded on Jesus Christ, a perfect foundation, and not Peter, a flawed and fallible one.

So what is the meaning of the pronouncement that Jesus made? A brief synopsis might suggest that Jesus was telling Peter and the other disciples that this collection of "rocks," knitted together to form the larger slab would be much like Paul's words in I Corinthians 12. Paul said, "The Spirit is not just an impersonal force or feeling; He is just as much a person within the trinity as the Father and the Son. Accordingly, the Spirit chooses where to impart gifts, as He works together with the Father and Son, to build up the church." That's the perspective that I want to build on.

Ephesians 2:19-22 says,

So then you are no longer foreigners and strangers, but fellow citizens with the saints, and members of God's household, built on the foundation of the apostles and prophets, with Christ Jesus Himself as the cornerstone. The whole building, being put together by Him, grows into a holy sanctuary in the Lord. You also are being built together for God's dwelling in the Spirit.

Peter himself, as an apostle, is understood by many to be this rock; the chief, though not the prince of the twelve. He was the senior among them, although not the superior over them. The church is built upon the foundation of the apostles. The first stones of that building were laid in and by their ministry; hence their names are said to be *written in the foundations* of the New Jerusalem. **See Footnote 2C, Page 56.**

Revelation 21:14 further states,

"And the wall of the city had twelve foundations, and in them the names of the twelve apostles of the Lamb."

Peter, being the apostle by whose hand the first stones of the church were laid, both in Jewish converts (Acts 2:1-47) and in the Gentile converts (Acts 10:1-48), might in some sense be said to be the rock on which it was built. This, however, hardly supports the notion that Peter is that rock. Peter had neither the headship as an apostle nor the authority to pass it on to his successors.

Others, by this *rock,* understand *Christ;* "*Thou art Peter,* thou hast the name of a *stone,* but *upon this rock,* pointing to himself, *I will build my church.*" When Jesus said, *"Destroy this temple, and in three days I will raise it up"* He was speaking of the temple of His body (John 2:19). This is explained in I Corinthians 3:11, and I Peter 2:6 –

There is, in fact, only one foundation, and no one can lay any foundation other than Jesus the Anointed.

For it is contained in Scripture: Look! I lay a stone in Zion, a chosen and honored cornerstone, and the one who believes in Him will never be put to shame!

Christ is both the Founder of the church and the Foundation; it is He who draws souls, and He draws them to Himself. To Him they are united, and upon Him they rest and have perpetual dependence, not upon Peter. Jesus acknowledged that Peter's confession was good and correct, *"Thou art the Christ, the Son of the living God,"* and the other disciples agreed with him. Jesus then follows that great revelation with this statement - *"this is the great truth upon which I will build My church."* If we take away this great truth, the universal church loses its support and falls to the ground. Furthermore, if Christ is not the Son of God, Christianity is a farce, and the church is a simple fantasy, preaching is in vain, our faith is in vain, and we all remain in our sins.

Confirmation is provided by Paul at I Corinthians 15:14-17 where he says –

If Christ has not been raised, then our proclamation is without foundation, and so is your faith. In addition, we are found to be false witnesses about God, because we have testified about God that He raised up Christ—whom He did not raise up if in fact the dead are not raised. For if the dead are not raised, Christ has not been raised. And if Christ has not been raised, your faith is worthless; you are still in your sins.

I searched within the Old and New Testament (KJV), and I discovered nearly 150 passages where the word rock was used. One hundred and thirty-nine of them referred to a physical rock. Eleven of them referenced a person. The person that all eleven verses referred to was God or Jesus. We know they are the same (John 1:1). In addition, the Hebrew meaning of the word rock is – firmness, stability, and faithfulness. Does that not describe our Savior? For sure, it does not personify Peter (Matthew 26:75). There's not much to gain by re-visiting the numerous passages that describe the common understanding of a rock. I do, however, think that there is value in listing the passages that depict Jesus and/or God as the rock. Deuteronomy 32:4, I Samuel 2:2, II Samuel 22:2 & 47, Psalm 18:2 & 31, Psalm 28:1, Psalm 31:3, Psalm 62:2, and Luke 6:48 which records these words –

If you work the words into your life, you will be like a man building a house, who dug deep and laid the foundation on the rock. When the flood came, the river crashed against that house and couldn't shake it, because it was built on the rock.

Christ promises to preserve and secure his church.

He assures us that *"The gates of hell shall not prevail against it."* The gates of hell shall not prevail against this great truth, and it will not prevail against the church which is built upon it. We must understand without a doubt, that the church does have enemies that war against it. They intend to corrupt, destroy, and overthrow the church. That's what Jesus means when He uses the phrase *"the gates of hell."* The gates of hell are the policies, practices, powers, and influences that the world uses to entice the interests of man. We must stay mindful of the fact that these attacks are not usually fleshly attacks. Paul reminds us in Ephesians 6:12, and Revelation 12:9 –

For we wrestle not against flesh and blood, but against principalities, against powers, against the rulers of the darkness of this world, against spiritual wickedness in high places.

And the great dragon was cast out, that old serpent, called the Devil, and Satan, which deceiveth the whole world: he was cast out into the earth, and his angels were cast out with him.

A collection of rocks that form a more effective and functional slab is what the church was meant to be. Jesus demonstrated this during His earthly ministry. He didn't go about randomly quoting scripture, setting up fund-raisers, or establishing annual days like usher's anniversaries or Men's Day services. Jesus utilized people and opportunities to make a difference in their lives. He accomplished that by building people up, restoring their integrity, and healing the impediments that hampered their ability to live constructive and productive lives. The church can effectively do the same today, but it will require a different approach.

God created man, and His purpose was, and continues to be, to have an intimate relationship with him. Romans 8:29-30 explains God's purpose for man.

God knew what he was doing from the very beginning. He decided from the outset to shape the lives of those who love him along the same lines as the life of his Son. The Son stands first in the line of humanity he restored. We see the original and intended shape of our lives there in him. After God made that decision of what his children should be like, he followed it up by calling people by name. After he called them by name, he set them on a solid basis with himself. And then, after getting them established, he stayed with them to the end, gloriously completing what he had begun.

He wants man to see Him as the Almighty God (Jehovah Elohim) who loves mankind and desires to lead, guide, protect, and provide for him. Man complicates this process by first, trying to navigate his own life and secondly, by creating for himself, other lesser gods. Therein is the beginning of the problems we see on vast display throughout our land. The good news is that this problem can be corrected. Sin and mankind's sinful nature are what brought us to where we are. God, however, provided a cure for this condition when He sacrificed His only begotten Son as a ransom and propitiation for our sin-nature. We have been given the opportunity to correct our relationship with Him by accepting the atoning sacrifice of His Son. **See Footnote 2D, Pages 56-57.**

John 3:16 says –

"For God expressed His love for the world in this way: He gave His only Son so that whoever believes in Him will not face everlasting destruction, but will have everlasting life."

Accepting the atoning sacrifice of Jesus Christ is just the beginning phase of inclusion into the Body of Christ (the Church). Finding contentment there perpetuates the current state of affairs in too many churches. The majority of its members are comfortably content with sitting in pews each week, while a minority of members are slowly and methodically wearing themselves out.

All churches belong to God, and consequently, all church members belong to Him as well. Church members (the Church) are the collective "rocks" that Jesus says create the larger slab when knitted together. God's commitment to protect the church from the destructive attacks of Satan is trustworthy, reliable, and consistent with His character. What that larger slab looks like weighs heavily on the church's willingness and commitment to follow God's divine plan.

The Old Testament confirms as it relates to the church, that its eminent purpose was given to particular persons who God declared were faithful and holy. Abraham and David are two individuals who acquired that distinction in the Old Testament. In the New Testament, Jesus ascribes this agency to Peter, but He does not in any way give him supreme authority over the church. The church is Christ's peculiar people, and they belong to him. The world is God's, and they that dwell therein; but the church is a chosen remnant that stands in relationship with God through Christ as our Mediator. The church displays His image and likeness. Psalm 24:1 reminds us of this fact.

The church is comprised of several believing men and women called out of the world, set apart from it, and therefore dedicated to the cause of Christ. It is not *our* church, it belongs to God. Peter conveys this truth in I Peter 5:2-4 when he admonished ministers to –

Feed the flock of God, not to lord it over God's people, and when the chief Shepherd shall appear, ye shall receive a crown of glory.

The Builder and Maker of the church is Christ himself. The church is the temple of God and Christ is the Builder (Zech. 6:11-13 & I Corinthians 6:19). By the power of the Holy Spirit through the preaching of his word, He adds souls to His church, and so builds it up with living stones, (1 Pet. 2:4-5). We are God's building and the building process is a progressive work. The foundation on which it is built is this Rock. It is incumbent upon us to let the architect do his part in developing the church by developing us. **See Footnote 2E, Page 57.**

The church is built upon a rock: a firm, strong, and lasting foundation which time will neither waste nor sink it under the weight of the building. Christ would not build his house upon the sand, for he knew that storms would arise. A rock is high, (Ps. 61:2). Christ's church does not stand upon a level with this world; a rock is large, and extends far, and so does the church's foundation; the larger and greater the rock, the stronger the foundation.

Footnotes - 2A-2E

Footnote 2A – The similarity between the church and an Embassy.

As Dr. Tony Evans so eloquently states, "there is an American Embassy in every recognized country in the world." Embassies are sovereign territories; they do not belong to the countries in which they reside; they belong to the countries they represent. Likewise, the church is supposed to be a little like heaven even though it is a long way from our heavenly home. The church is supposed to be that place where troubled people can go and find hope, truth, acceptance, justice, safety, and freedom.

In many ways, the church has lost its resemblance of God's kingdom perspective. The impact of the church has diminished not only inside the church but also in the surrounding community. The contemporary purpose of the church is to be a model for the world. The church must operate in the world while providing an alternative to the world. "When the church functions as a divine structure operating in a liberating manner according to the way God has ordained it to be, the church sets itself apart as a haven, similar to an embassy," adds Dr. Evans.

Footnote 2B – The meaning of Petra

When Jesus said, "Upon this rock, I will build My church," He used the Greek word "Petra," which means a collection of rocks, knitted together to form a larger slab. Thus, Jesus's church would be comprised of His unified followers who would confess Him as the Christ, the Son of the living God, just as Peter did. Jesus's message to Peter reinforces two points. The first is that the church is comprised of committed followers of Christ. He conveys the message that we not only make-up the church, we are also the church. The second message is that we all have individual talents, gifts, and purpose that collectively complete the body of Christ, the church. Paul reminds us in 1 Corinthians 12:12 and Romans 12:5 -

For as the body is one and has many parts, and all the parts of that body, though many, are one body—so also is Christ.

In the same way we who are many are one body in Christ and individually members of one another.

Petra, the collection of rocks, represents the aggregation of believers that collectively make up the church.

Footnote 2C – The churches foundation

The church is built upon the foundation of the apostles. The first stones of that building were laid in and by their ministry. Jesus was the originator and orchestrator of that ministry. He was also the object of their instruction. They, along with everyone else that overcomes, will have their names *written in the foundations* of the New Jerusalem.

I will make him that overcomes, a pillar in the temple of my God, and he shall go no more out: and I will write upon him the name of my God, and the name of the city of my God, which is new Jerusalem, which cometh down out of heaven from my God: and I will write upon him My new name.

Footnote 2D – God's desire for mankind

God's desire is for man to see Him as the Almighty God (Jehovah Elohim) who loves mankind and desires to lead, guide, protect, and provide for him. He sacrificed His only begotten Son as a ransom and propitiation for our sin-nature. We have been given the opportunity to correct our relationship with Him by accepting the atoning sacrifice of His Son.

If you confess with your mouth, "Jesus is Lord," and believe in your heart that God raised Him from the dead, you will be saved. One believes with the heart, resulting in righteousness and one confesses with the mouth, resulting in salvation. The Scripture says that everyone who believes on Him will not be put to shame. *Romans 10:9-11*

Footnote 2E – The Builder of the church

The Builder and Maker of the church is Christ himself. John 1:1-4 and Acts 2:46-47 says,

In the beginning was the Word and the Word was with God, and the Word was God. He was with God in the beginning. All things were created through Him, and apart from Him not one thing was created that has been created.

Day after day they met in the temple [area] continuing with one mind, and breaking bread in various private homes. They were eating their meals together with joy and generous hearts, praising God continually, and having favor with all the people. And the Lord kept adding to their number daily those who were being saved.

Chapter 3
The Church's Purpose
and Intent

I am writing you these instructions so that, if I am delayed, you will know how people ought to conduct themselves in God's household, which is the church of the living God, the pillar and foundation of the truth.

I Timothy 3:14-15

The church is the regenerate people of God, saved by the power of God, for the intended purposes of God in this world. Jesus asserted that the building or structuring of the church is something He would do personally. He said, *"Upon this rock, I will build my church"* (Matthew 16:18). That statement however, did not mean that He would not use called-out people to carry out that task. As stated earlier in this book, the church is not the building; it is the body of called-out believers. This simply means that the body of believers is still the church, even after they exit the building or edifice used to worship God. Everything we think, say, and do, should be done from the perspective of blood-bought believers, representing the Jesus we place our faith in.

Paul said at Romans 12:4-5,

For just as each of us has one body with many members, and these members do not all have the same function, so in Christ we, though many, form one body, and each member belongs to all the others.

Every believer has a unique and specific function in the church. It is unfair when believers take the position that the clergy or the leadership of the church has the responsibility for funding, managing, and maintaining all of the ministries of the church and the laypeople receive all of the benefits derived from them. A believer that positions himself as the maximum authority over the church unilaterally appropriates the position that only Jesus should hold.

Jesus backed up His words, teachings, and expectations by His personal example. His death, burial, and overwhelming resurrection serve as vindication and approval of all he did. He called, mentored, and developed twelve ordinary men to be model leaders of His teachings. He taught them the message they were to proclaim, that teaching was founded on Godly principle, and steeped in the biblical word of God. Prior to departure, He assured them that the Holy Spirit would guide them on their journey. **See Footnote 3A, Page 70.**

The early church or Christian community gathered together for the breaking of bread. As they told and retold stories of Jesus Christ, they recalled the things He said, the behavior He exhibited, the attitude He demonstrated, and the powerful works He performed. As a result, many of the apostles were also producing similar signs and wonders that Jesus performed.

The community continually committed themselves to learning what the apostles taught them, gathering for fellowship, breaking bread, and praying. Everyone felt a sense of awe because the apostles were doing many signs and wonders among them.

Acts 2:42-43

Jesus intended for every believer to be equipped with the spiritual tools needed to fulfill their God-given purpose. He also provided, through demonstration, the attitude, behavior, and methods to reflect Christian principles and practices in their day-to-day morals and civility. God expects the church to focus holistically in all that we think, say, and do.

All of Scripture is God-breathed; in its inspired voice, we hear useful teaching, rebuke, correction, instruction, and training for a life that is right, so that God's people may be up to the task ahead and have all they need to accomplish every good work.

II Timothy 3:16-17

I listened to a panel discussion recently where a pastor stated that too many parishioners expect the church to address all of their life's issues and concerns. He said that the leadership of the church is only responsible for addressing their spiritual concerns. I agree that man's spiritual concerns should be the priority of the church. However, I believe that "all" aspects of a parishioner's life should be addressed within the church. If the church does not equip the saints with spiritual guidelines, even as they relate to civil life, where else should they find these qualities? **See Footnote 3B, Pages 70-71.**

Leadership, and especially pastoring, is not an endeavor that should be segmented to only provide Godly counsel but not include the whole man. Our Christian walk is not limited to our conduct in church. Our work, our family, our politics, and all extra-curricular activities impact our credibility and relationship with God.

The church is the body of Christ—a group of people unified under Christ, who represent and reflect Him to the world. The purpose of the church is to join people, men and women of different backgrounds and talents, and provide them training and opportunities for God's work. This is accomplished internally, within the body, and externally, in the world. Ephesians 4 is a great example of this. Teaching the doctrine of Christ is heavily recommended.

However, within that teaching, we are admonished to walk within the world while utilizing Godly principles - not as the world operates. I Corinthians 12 reminds us that we are many members but one body. There will be a conglomerate of personalities, issues, concerns, and challenges within the congregation, but what better place to properly address them than the church. Church leadership is a divine calling, and it's not for the faint of heart.

You might recall Paul addressing immoral issues within the church of Corinth (I Corinthians 5) where he advised the leadership to properly address that issue and correct it. He also provided instructions on how to go about doing it. The objective of sound teaching and unifying the body is to encourage the members of the church to take care of each other. The church provides a place to do just that. The church provides us an opportunity to bring each other's needs before the body and pray for God's direction.

Jesus's intent for the church is to show support for one another through honoring, encouraging, loving, and showing compassion for each other. That's how we meet the practical needs of each other. James 1:27 says to us - *Real, and true religion, from God the Father's perspective, is about caring for the orphans and widows who suffer needlessly and resisting the evil influence of the world.* That level of caring is not limited to widows and orphans; it's any need that we observe that we can make an impact on.

Even though some will take advantage of the assistance that the church often provides, one of the purposes of the church is to provide for the needs of its members. God intended that every able body work and meet the needs of their family and the family of God. Paul was a tentmaker, Jesus was a carpenter, and many of the disciples were fishermen. Albeit, the church is still the best opportunity to reconcile differences and right wrongs between our interactions with fellow believers. Paul says at Acts 20:33-35 -

Remember my example: I never once coveted a single coin of silver or gold. I never looked twice at someone's fine clothing. No, you know this: I worked with my own two hands making tents, and I paid my own expenses and my companions' expenses as well. This is my last gift to you, this example of a way of life: a life of hard work, a life of helping the weak, a life that echoes every day those words of Jesus our King, who said, "It is more blessed to give than to receive."

Even if we don't have the financial ability to help or assist in meeting someone's needs, one of the most powerful means of assistance we can provide is to collectively keep each other lifted to God in prayer. When we selflessly bring each other's needs before God, He will orchestrate who or what's needed to rectify the situation. That's what the early church did, and it still works today.

Every time you cross my mind, I break out in exclamations of thanks to God. Each exclamation is a trigger to prayer. I find myself praying for you with a glad heart. I am so pleased that you have continued on in this with us, believing and proclaiming God's Message, from the day you heard it right up to the present. There has never been the slightest doubt in my mind that the God who started this great work in you would keep at it and bring it to a flourishing finish on the very day Christ Jesus appears.

Philippians 1:3-6

The intent of the church (the body of believers) is to establish a foundation for an organized spiritual family of believers. Within this family, God brings about the unity of the spirit while recognizing and utilizing the vastly differing gifts, talents, and personalities. As maturation develops within the church, believers are equipped to properly care for each other and extend care and empathy for the world around us. God said in Genesis 2:18 – **"It is not good that the man should be alone; I will make a helper suitable for him."** *God made man to be a social creation. Socialization is how man grows and develops. Even God socialized with man daily; thereby establishing a relationship between man, woman, and Him. We are still socially created and grow, care, and comfort comes about through our interaction with each other.*

In the same way that iron sharpens iron, a person sharpens the character of his friend. Proverbs 27:17

The purpose of the church is to be the believer's spiritual family. It is through the church that God takes people with different personalities and gifts, unifies them as a single body, and equips them to care for each other to reach the world. We discover our calling and purpose through our relationship with God, and by surrounding ourselves with accurate biblical teaching and a loving church community.

Jesus emphasized the Church's purpose and intent when He stated its great command and commission. He said that the great command of the church is to –

Love your God, with all your heart, with all your soul, with all your mind, and with all your strength. The second great commandment is this: "Love others in the same way you love yourself." There are no commandments more important than these.
                                                    Mark 12:30-31

He further stated that the external purpose of the church is to introduce Christ to the world. He says at Matthew 28:18-20 that the church is to –

Go therefore, and make disciples of all nations, baptizing them in the name of the Father and of the Son and of the Holy Spirit, teaching them to observe everything I have commanded you. And remember, I am with you always, even to the end of the age."

This means that whether we witness to those within our neighborhoods, community, or in foreign lands, we are manifesting the embodiment of the Holy Spirit in us. The church is called to expose the character of Jesus by telling others about Him. If you are a Christian, you have become a part of God's earthly Kingdom and your King is Jesus. This King Jesus is our Savior. He died for us, rose from the dead, and through our faith in Him, our sins are forgiven. In doing so, we receive eternal life.

Learning what God intended for the church is critically dependent upon how He provides the tools necessary to accomplish it. The Bible provides the details of what's needed. The commitment to learning, understanding, and applying those tools and principles is how the church becomes effective in ministry. The most powerful message He provides is "everything by faith and through the power of the Holy Spirit."

The writer of Hebrews says it this way, *"Without faith it is impossible to please God, for the one who draws near to Him must believe that He exists and rewards those who seek Him." Hebrews 11:6.* If you continue reading the remainder of Hebrews Chapter 11, you will see all of the great accomplishments of others throughout the scriptures, BY FAITH! Faith in whom, or in what, you might ask. Before His departure, Jesus assured His disciples and us, with these words –

If you love me, show it by doing what I've told you. I will talk to the Father, and he'll provide you another Comforter so that you will always have someone with you. This Comforter is the Holy Spirit of Truth. The godless world can't understand him because it doesn't have eyes to see him, and doesn't know what to look for. But you know him already because he has been staying with you, and will always be in you!
John 14:16-17

Even Jesus ministered in the power of the Holy Spirit. The Holy Spirit is the medium by which we are born anew and gain access into the kingdom of God (John 3). The Holy Spirit is the one common denominator that unifies believers. It is the Holy Spirt that empowers believers and produces the common focus for the advancement of the body of Christ – the Church. The church is the medium that God uses today to display to the world what it looks like to live under a righteous government, ruled by a sovereign King.

As believers, and as the body of Christ, the church, we have a responsibility to live our lives in a way that reflects to the world what it means to live under the rule of our sovereign King, Jesus the Christ. When the world sees us and our interaction with others, they should see the same example that Jesus demonstrated when He interacted with others. We must follow His lead. He commanded us to love one another, and in doing so, others would know that we are His disciples (John 13:35).

Everyone who professes to know Christ ought to do their absolute best to make the local church a living, breathing example of what it means to live a life surrendered to Christ. We are the light of the world, a city sitting on a hill for the world to see. That is God's purpose and intent for the church. He wants to show the world His unlimited power and His unconditional love through His Church. What does the world see when it focuses on you? **See Footnote 3C, Pages 71-72.**

Footnotes - 3A-3C

Footnote 3A – Ordinary Men and Women

In the book, *Twelve Ordinary Men*, John MacArthur expounds on how Jesus called 12 ordinary men from various backgrounds to mentor them as disciples. Their humanity was revealed throughout their three year tutelage. Peter would often put his foot in his mouth, Thomas was referred to as the doubter, James and John sought to be seated to Jesus's right and left in glory, and Judas, who committed the greatest sin of all in his betrayal of our Lord.

The bigger point is simply this, none of these men possessed any special or professional skill or talent. They were 12 ordinary men, but they were going to be used to impact the world in an extraordinary way. What is most unique and powerful is not who they were; it was all about *Who* called them to this ministry. It's the same for us today. God can and will use anyone He deems usable.

Footnote 3B – Equipping the saints.

So Christ himself gave the apostles, the prophets, the evangelists, the pastors and teachers, to equip his people for works of service, so that the body of

Christ may be built up until we all reach unity in the faith and in the knowledge of the Son of God and become mature, attaining to the whole measure of the fullness of Christ.

Ephesians 4:11-13

The word of God provides instruction for every aspect of our daily lives *(II Timothy 3:16)*. The church is comprised of common everyday men and women who are fallible, as are those outside of the church body. The difference, however, is that the church has the power of God and the workings of the Holy Spirit at its disposal. Therefore, within the church, there should be the highest level of character, trust, and integrity. If the church does not equip the saints with spiritual guidelines, even as they relate to civil life and morality, where else should believers find these qualities?

Footnote 3C – What does the world see?

I was told about a church building that burned to the ground. As people in the community were gathering around the burning edifice, someone asked, how will this tragedy affect the community and how does it affect you? The person responded, "not at all!" When asked to explain, the response was, "this church has been in the community for 40 years and this is the first time I have ever seen any fire come out of it."

What a sad commentary. When a church has been in a community for a number of years and there is nothing impactful that the community can say about its significance, people may begin to question its relevance in the community.

Chapter 4
Obstacles *and* Challenges

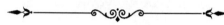

Be prepared. You're up against far more than you can handle on your own. Take all the help you can get, every weapon God has issued, so that when it's all over but the shouting, you'll still be on your feet.

Ephesians 6:13

Again, we are discussing various aspects of church and the declaration that Jesus made in Matthew 16 where He stated that His church is built upon a rock and the gates of hell would never prevail against it. Within this chapter, we will be exploring the various challenges relating to the gates of hell. Although we have the assurance that the gates of hell will not prevail, we would be remiss not to prepare ourselves for the attacks that will attempt to derail the effect that the church can, and should have in and on the world around us.

One could argue that the top challenges for the church are equally challenging for pastors. In a 2023 study conducted by Barna Group and Moody, ten challenges were identified as top concerns for pastors and, in essence, the church. They identified them as -

1. Mobilizing for evangelism
2. Concern for evangelism
3. Retaining young adults
4. Leadership burnout
5. Member mobilization
6. Effects of social media
7. Member bible knowledge
8. Present-day sexual ethics
9. Member indifference
10. Community outreach

Paul states in Ephesians 6 that the real battles and dangers we face are not against flesh and blood. He reminds us that the enemies we see are real enough, but they are stimulated by spiritual forces of darkness that stay cleverly hidden from view. These forces often reveal themselves as institutional evils, annihilation, terror, cruelty, and oppression. He admonishes us to utilize the wisdom obtained from the word of God as effective weapons to combat these forces. We are told to stand firm in the power of God by putting on the whole armor of God. Paul acknowledges that although Satan and his demons are ultimately destined for destruction, they are formable foes that must be dealt with. Until they are destroyed, we must apply God's

Word and be consistent in our prayers to Him.

Let's take a brief look at the findings from the Barna Group and Moody study. Mobilizing for evangelism should be a viable component within every church. God's people have been called to be on mission with God. Mobilization is all about ensuring that God's people, in every generation, join with Him in a viable effort for mission work to the people of the world. The importance of the ministry of mobilization is critical and extremely counter-productive when omitted.

Concern for evangelism is not only connected to mobilization but should also be at the heart of every believer. Once we have been called out of the world's darkness and exposed to the light of the world, why wouldn't we want to share it with as many people as possible? How we accomplish this requires teaching, training, and discipling (*helping others to become more like Jesus, by teaching them how to grow in their faith*), but the desire to share it should be within the heart of believers.

Retaining young adults is vital to the continuation of the church's legacy. The success of the church is greatly dependent on the efforts of the church body. As members transition into adults and one day, seniors, there needs to be capable and qualified younger folk ready and willing to continue the necessary ministries that seek out, recruit, minister to, and disciple others to keep the torch lit and the fire burning in the heart of the church.

Leadership burnout is an obvious expectation when only a small minority of the church is attempting to fulfill the expectations of the entire church body. Leaders must be attentive to these needs while searching for mentees within the church body. Leaders must be willing to allow prospective new leaders to utilize their talents and gifts with the understanding that every believer is different. The message utilized in the training must be Bible-based and supported, but the method will often reflect some differentiation.

Member mobilization is the ultimate goal. Every member has something to offer and should be encouraged to grow, develop, and participate. I recall one pastor sharing his method of member mobilization and participation. During the New member's orientation, new members would have to choose where they wanted to serve in ministry.

Included in the orientation was a period of time spent in street ministry. If they didn't choose a ministry by the time the orientation was completed, they would be placed in the street ministry. Street ministry can be quite challenging, and most new members were intimidated at the prospect. Therefore, almost all new members would have a chosen ministry of their liking by the completion of the orientation. He was not forcing them into a ministry, but he explained to them that he had an obligation from God to equip the saints. I agree.

The effects of social media are making drastic

changes to the church environment. We are all aware that *digital platforms* provide one of the greatest opportunities to engage with your congregation, for people evaluating your church, and for those who don't yet know Jesus. Photographer Steven Estes recently stated that *"Social media has the potential to be the greatest tool to advance the gospel since the printing press. It basically gives the average person a pulpit (or platform) from which to share the gospel like never before. It also gives churches a constant connection to their congregants beyond a Sunday morning service. It's up to us whether or not we use it as such."*

While social media has blessed both our church community and thousands of others around the world, it's also a reason for great concern. In 2020, the Netflix film *The Social Dilemma* explored this perceived tension and exposed some of the troubling realities of a digital world. The film revealed that social media can be a breeding ground for comparison, contempt, hatred, and division. Studies show that social media usage often increases anxiety and feelings of low self-worth. Social media is a tool to be used, but it can also be a tool that can easily use us. The church needs to better understand how social media can shape opinions, perceptions, and politics. Social media is impactful. It can be a blessing, and it can be destructive.

The church needs to develop an effective process that details how it will implement and utilize social media productively. The church needs to better understand how social media can shape opinions, perceptions, and politics. The church must resolve to be shaped by Jesus's love, grace, truth, Word, and worship—and then to use social media to bless others through the use of it.

Jesus and his disciples never shied away from controversy or danger; instead, they went to public places and reached out to people in the middle of chaos. They met people right where they were and sought to share hope with all of them. The church needs to look like Jesus in all settings. The church must shine the light of Christ wherever people are - for the glory of God and the good of all people.

Member Bible knowledge, or really, the lack of, is too often a challenge within the church. Missions, witnessing, teaching, leading, and discipling all suffer when members lack knowledge and maturity in the faith they are offering or inviting others to become a participant. Paul reminds us at II Timothy 3:16 that the word of God is applicable to our total development. He also tells us at II Timothy 2:15 that our study is what enables us to obtain God's approval and effectiveness in our walk. Teaching, training, and mentoring for effective disciple-building require time, patience, and wisdom.

Present-day sexual ethics is a huge concern for churches today. Sexual challenges have always been a struggle for the church, and today, the expansion of ideals, perception, and beliefs have gotten beyond *out of control.*

One of the greatest weaknesses in the church today is that too many fail to believe that God invests His power in the Word of God, the Bible. Too many churches are looking for power in a program, in a scheme, a shiny object, anything and everything but the infallible word of God. Well, the infallible word of God is the best place to find the answer. Church conflict occurs when people within the congregation put their personal ideas, beliefs, thoughts, and motives above and before the betterment of the church.

Member indifference is not what Jesus taught, and it can destroy the effectiveness within a church if is allowed to go unchecked. Believers must pay close attention to the warning signs and protect themselves from the poison of indifference. Indifference is defined as a lack of interest, concern, sympathy, or unimportance. Jesus taught us to love one another and He said by this, others will know that you are My disciples (John 13:35). Love is not the opposite of hate, faith is not the opposite of heresy, and life is not the opposite of death. The opposite of love, faith, and life is indifference.

In the third chapter of Revelation, John addresses seven churches. He provides praise, warnings, and encouragement to them, with the exception of the church of Laodicea. In verse 15, he tells them – *they are neither hot nor cold, and He wishes that they were one or the other.* When it comes to spiritual matters, members who are hot are involved and committed to their faith. They dedicate quality time with Jesus, studying, praying, and listening to Him; obedience usually follows. Being cold to spiritual matters is not a good thing, but it's not the worst either. Being cold at least positions a person where a faithful spiritual encounter can totally impact them and produce a transformative change.

The challenge for lukewarm people as it relates to spiritual matters is that it produces indifference. They possess just enough Bible knowledge to negate resistance, but not enough real faith to become completely engaged. There is much more difficulty in converting a lukewarm person (*indifferent*) than it is a cold person. In verse 16, John says that God will vomit a lukewarm person out of His mouth. Indifferent believers are destructive to the church. **See Footnote 4A, Page 83.**

Community outreach is what Jesus taught, what the disciples emulated, and what Paul demonstrated. A community outreach initiative focuses on programs, activities, and services whose aim is to make a productive impact within the community outside of the church. There will likely be benefits from them that the church will realize, but its primary focus should be towards making a difference in the lives of individuals within the community, whether members or non-members of the church.

Community outreach provides an opportunity for

the church to reveal to the community what areas the church has interest in, from a holistic perspective. It provides opportunity for the church to engage with the community to learn what concerns they may have in order to partner with them in brainstorming potential efforts toward resolution. Community outreach also provides an opportunity for the church to extend a welcoming hand of fellowship, love, and support to its neighbors.

One of the most important characteristics of the church is to show itself as an asset to the community and to reflect a persona that doesn't model the world. This is one area where the entire church can get involved in a variety of ways to expose the church to the community, learn more about the community, and grow and develop in mission ministry. This ministry is usually not the most popular within the church, but it can become the most impactful. The greater the training and development, the smoother and more effective it will be. This is an area of training that engages the "who, what, when, how, and why training. **See Footnote 4B, Pages 83-84.**

Another source of church conflict involves anger, hate, and/or hurt. The trademark of the church and its most effective means of ministering to the world is demonstrated when it reflects the love of God, as Jesus modeled. That means that today's leaders must take on the challenge of replacing the destructive ancestral policies and processes that too many hold. If believers, disciples, and congregants are going to be effective in their mission endeavors, they will have to embrace the ideas that Jesus taught.

This kind of love extends beyond and outside of cultural, political, racial, economical, regional, sexual, and ideological lines. The church of God must model diversity, truth, generosity, flexibility, morality, and community. All of these characteristics must be anchored in righteousness. No church will be perfect in exhibiting these traits, but all churches should buttress these initiatives with the righteous principles and practices provided within the Bible. **See Footnote 4C, Pages 84-85.**

Matthew Chapter 18, verses 15-16 encourages members to *settle their differences with each other privately. If your brother sins against you, go and tell him his fault between you and him alone. If he hears you, you have gained a brother. If this fails, seek help in resolving the dispute.* What will not fix the problem is neglect, avoidance, or abandoning the situation. Issues unattended will only worsen. When challenges of any sort are consistently resolved utilizing the Word of God, even if it takes a while to get the affected parties back to some sort of normalcy, good outcomes are more likely to happen because God's Word, principles, and practices are more effective than anything else we can use. **See footnote 4D, Pages 85-87.**

Footnotes - 4A-4D

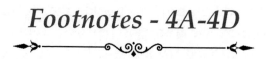

Footnote 4A – Indifference

In the third chapter of Revelation, God equates being lukewarm with indifference. Lukewarm is like straddling a fence. It depicts people who won't commit to any position. The challenge for lukewarm people, as it relates to spiritual matters, is that it produces indifference. They possess just enough Bible knowledge to negate resistance, but not enough real faith to become completely engaged. The church (the Body of Christ) must be composed of people that are willing to stand for what God says is right, even when the majority takes a different stance.

Footnote 4B – Community mission ministry

Some of the most important characteristics of the church are to show itself as an asset to the community and to reflect a persona that doesn't model the world. The word of God says in I Peter 2:9 –

But you are a chosen people, a royal priesthood, a holy nation, God's special possession, that you may declare the praises of him who called you out of darkness into his wonderful light.

God has chosen men and women that are *in the world*, to live in the world as a light that reflects a lifestyle that differs from the world's manner of life. He reminds us that we are a chosen people, demonstrating the royalty of God in holiness. God's people are to declare all praises to the God that brought them out of the world's darkness and replaced it with His illuminating light. When the church projects this illumination light in the community, the power of God is seen and the community is impacted.

Footnote 4C – Diversity, truth, and flexibility

The church of God must model diversity, truth, generosity, flexibility, morality, and community. However, all of these characteristics must be anchored in righteousness. The unchurched today may not look like the unchurched of past years. The litany of reasons people choose not to be a part of the organized church today is much greater and more sophisticated.

Church hurt, gender challenges, political differences, and personal past experiences require a more compassionate approach when witnessing to them. I'm not suggesting that the church compromise or water down the truth of God's righteousness, but seasoning it with empathy is a good recipe for success. Jesus demonstrated this kind of compassion with the woman caught in Adultery. In John Chapter 8, He says in verses 7-11,

Jesus said to them, "Let any one of you who is without sin be the first to throw a stone at her." Again he

stooped down and wrote on the ground. At this, those who heard began to go away one at a time, the older ones first, until only Jesus was left, with the woman still standing there. Jesus straightened up and asked her, "Woman, where are they? Has no one condemned you?" "No one, sir," she said. "Then neither do I condemn you," Jesus declared. "Go now and leave your life of sin."

Footnote 4D – Difficult, but right!

In I Corinthians 5, Paul confronted a serious issue that was not taking place within the church, and it was not being addressed.

Because of my deep love for you, I must express my concern about the report brought to me regarding the lewd and immoral behavior exhibited in your community. This scandal has come to my attention because this kind of thing is unheard of even among the outsiders around us: I understand a man is having sexual relations with his father's wife. You have turned into an arrogant lot who refuse to see the tragedy right in front of your eyes and mourn for it. If you would face these hard realities, the one living in this sin would be removed from the community. I direct you to release this man over to Satan so his rebellious nature will be destroyed and his spirit might be rescued in the day the Lord Jesus returns.

I Corinthians 5:1,2 & 5

A pastor that I have a great deal of respect for told of an experience he had when he was pastoring a small congregation. He admitted that they were often challenged with their finances. One Sunday, a well-off couple became members of their church body and became close friends with him and his wife. Every Sunday, this couple would take him and his wife to dinner after service. They began making large donations to the church. This was great, as those financial challenges soon disappeared.

Then one Sunday while at dinner, the man began to suggest changes that he thought would be good for the church. The pastor explained how he implemented changes, but it was not received well. The couple threatened to leave if their ideas were not considered. The pastor wrestled with this. He did not agree with the changes they were proposing, but he had never felt the financial comfort and ease that came with their financial contributions. Thankfully, he trusted God and told them that he would not implement their wishes. So, they eventually left the church.

The financial struggles were back, but they managed to stay afloat. Within the next several months, the church continued to grow in numbers. Three of those new families were professional people (a doctor, lawyer, and a construction contractor). None of the three took him and his wife to dinner each Sunday, but they became huge donors, not only in their giving during service but also for special projects they had on hold while waiting for the finances to support them.

The message is – God has instructed us to come to Him when we're burdened *(Matthew 11:28)*. He wants us to lean on, depend on, and trust Him, and when the time is right *(Kairos time)*, He will bring it to pass *(Proverbs 3:4-5)*.

Chapter 5
Church Finances *and* Budgeting

Surely you know that those who work at the Temple get their food from the Temple. And those who serve at the altar get part of what is offered at the altar. It is the same with those who have the work of telling the Good News. The Lord has commanded that those who tell the Good News should get their living from this work.

I Corinthians 9:13-14

In our society, Churches are recognized as the pillars of spiritual growth and as vital contributors to community development. In addition, it is the church through its effectiveness in money management that enables them to successfully implement those operations and expansions. Acquiring these funds can be challenging enough, but proper management of them is critical. How the Church manages its finances is about more than keeping the lights on; it's about fulfilling its mission to serve the Church and community, elevate the spirituality of its members, and transform the lives of its members and the community in which it resides in the process.

The strategies utilized by the Church to accomplish this will determine its effectiveness, influence, and sustainability as it endeavors to identify, address, and impact the various ills within its targeted area. Managing and reassessing these strategies will govern how long they will be able to maintain their effort within the community. The Church, like any other organization, religious or secular, needs money to carry out its missions. Unlike secular organizations, the Church does not sell a product; it offers its services free of charge, but it is supported through free-will offerings and contributions.

It should be clearly understood that church money and other church resources belong to the church, and not to any individual, including pastors! The financial contributions of members of a church are meant to meet the needs and obligations in the church. It intends to assist the church as it strives to accomplish its mission and vision. Offerings are given in church with the faith that they will be used honestly and transparently to meet the needs in the house of God. Church funds are public funds held in trust, and they should be managed with the highest level of accountability and morality.

The first step towards enforcing accountability in the management of church finance is to ensure that church money is overseen and managed by more than one reputable person appointed by the church for that purpose. Church money should not be controlled by a single person but managed by a committee of people with good reputations, men and women filled with the Holy Spirit and wisdom who have been proven trustworthy in prior engagements. That was the recommendation of the original apostles when there was a complaint about how church resources were being used at the church's inception.

In Acts 4:35-37, it is clearly stated that – *"Those who lead in spiritual matters should also take the lead in financial matters."* Most Churches establish a financial committee that consists of people with a financial background and are trustworthy stewards with integrity. The finance committee as a whole is tasked with generating and maintaining church funds to support the organization. The committee is responsible for maintaining and auditing the church's financial records, and they must make decisions that will directly affect the church's finances. The funds of the church should be handled in such a way that is defensible against any accusations.

For accountability, church offerings should not be paid into a private account. It should not be the personal account of a pastor or any church member. The church should have dedicated bank accounts for various offerings, which should be managed by the committee responsible for the administration of various projects in the church.

In the Old Testament, the three-yearly tithes were

not taken to the private houses of individual Priests or Levites but were brought to storehouses in various cities in Israel. Then, they were collected and administered by Levites (*who were administrative assistants to the Priests*), with distributions made to Priests, Levites, widows, the fatherless, the poor, and strangers in the land of Israel. This should be the pattern for collection, storage, and distribution or utilization of church funds and other resources.

In the New Testament, financial contributions to the church were not used by the apostles alone to finance excessive lifestyles, while the other members of the church suffered in poverty and need. Rather, distributions were made according to people's needs in the church. Utilizing this method, no one lacked in the church.

Another important factor regarding financial accountability in the church is the understanding that church funds are not just meant for the upkeep of pastors alone. Church funds are meant to address all church needs and meet all needs that arise in the house of God. Those financial contributions should not only include taking care of the ministers of the gospel but also intended to provide for the maintenance of the poor and needy, widows, the fatherless, and others who need assistance. In addition, it should include efforts to finance programs aimed at spreading the gospel. Lastly, but equally important, it is also used to maintain the places of worship.

True accountability with the church finances will only occur when church funds are used to solve all problems in the church, not just to take care of pastors while the flocks suffer! Ministers will be called to account for the way they took care of the flocks under their care, spiritually and otherwise, with the resources available at their disposal.

A common question that's often asked is – How much should I give to the church, and is tithing biblically supported for today's church? The tithe was a tax levied on Israelites that supported the Levites. I have not found any specific evidence that it was prescribed for Christians. The church should not demand that its people tithe. However, there is nothing wrong in utilizing 10 percent (a tithe) as a guide for consistent giving. God encourages us to give from the heart – a cheerful heart. The law mandated 10 percent. Grace should compel us to give at least as much as the law requires. I do believe that whatever agreed upon method the church uses, those in leadership should model that level of giving.

Tithing is a concept that has to be taught. If your church's method of teaching tithing is simply reading the instructions given by Malachi and Luke, the giving might be more from compulsion than from the heart. If this is your method, it should be made clear to visitors that this is not an obligation placed on their giving. It should be made clear that even if they choose not to give, it's acceptable. If they begin attending the church or participate in the education and training programs, the who, the why, and the how, as it relates to tithing can be shared then. It is always a good practice to teach and explain doctrinal issues and concerns when there's an opportunity for questions and answers.

Tithing originated in the Old Testament (Numbers 18:21). Tithing represented a tenth of an individual's income, symbolizing not just their financial support but also their devotion, obedience, and trust in God. This practice was not simply transactional; it was a covenantal act, portraying the relationship of trust and honor between God and the believer. In the New Testament, Paul's teachings moved from a focus on the amount of the gift to the attitude behind their giving.

Paul emphasized that each person is to give what they purposed in their heart to give. He explained that our giving should not be reluctantly given or given under compulsion. He concluded that God loves a cheerful giver. Paul further conveys the point that givers must transition from the Old Testament view of tithing to a heartfelt expression of their generosity, which he says, reflects the believer's relationship and devotion to God. I ask, should our giving now be less than what was required in the Old Testament? We must understand that it's not the amount of giving that matters most. It is the sincerity and the sacrifice behind it. **See Footnote 5A, Page 103.**

Whatever method the church decides to use for funding the church, consistency in following it is a must. The money that flows through the church is used to support its operations and to fund all other financial responsibilities of the church, including staff salaries, ministry activities, maintaining the infrastructure of the church, community engagement activities, and the salaries of church leaders. Good financial management of the church requires financially astute managers with integrity, commitment, and the knowledge necessary to properly manage those funds.

As challenging as that can be at times, these managers must adhere to and follow the vision and mission established by the leadership. The vision and mission of the church might be determined by the Pastor, a board, the church body, or any combination of the three. Churches that fail to incorporate these practices often suffer. God's church was meant to thrive, not just survive. That is one of the many reasons why proper vetting of those selected to pastor is such a critical and important component to church success.

Prioritizing the factors in the selection of a pastor may vary, based on the specific situation, needs, and objectives of the church. If someone, or a committee, is developing a church plant, the person selected as pastor/leader is usually pre-determined. A general idea of what the church will focus on and its approach to get there are usually parsed out in the organizing stages. What often is not yet fully developed is the complete role of the pastor/leader.

The selection process for established churches is

often more detailed because the typical search is for someone with the credentials and skillset to continue a role that has been vacated. With both scenarios, the focus should extend beyond the present and extend to a forward-thinking perspective that includes where the church is anticipating its future endeavors to embrace.

My philosophy is that it *is better to aim high and temporarily settle for something lower than to set your initial aim too low.* The expansive wish list for your pastor selection may be undiscoverable, unaffordable, or maybe even unreasonable, but having more information than is needed is much simpler to manage than not having enough.

The church today is in a period of extreme diversification. There is great debate over what real healthy and constructive pastoral leadership looks like. What are the qualities a pastor needs to be successful and effective? What can church members do to partner with and better understand pastors to produce a healthier church family and environment? Many pastors are not finding success and fruitfulness. Not because their calling is questionable, but because their methods are. Pastors and the body of Christ must collectively put a biblically-based plan together for the church and follow it.

God's word, God's plan, and God's purpose will never fail. We just have to align ourselves with His word and stay the course. That's how we help those who have been called into pastoral leadership to be successful. That's how we help churches to have the best chance of being a healthy church under the leadership of effective pastors. **See Footnote 5B, Page 103.**

When searching for the right person to serve as pastor of the church, the focus should be on finding a person who has leadership skills, people skills, and empathy for God's people. Pastors must be able to decipher God's word and be committed to teaching sound doctrine. They must possess a solid understanding of the gospel, conversion, and evangelism. They must be committed to utilizing a biblical understanding of church membership and church discipline. Simply put, they must love God, love God's people, and reflect the love of God in all decision-making.

Paul says in Romans 1:16-17 –

I am not the least bit embarrassed about the gospel. I won't shy away from it, because it is God's power to save every person who believes: first the Jew, and then the non-Jew. You see, in the good news, God's restorative justice is revealed. And as we will see, it begins with and ends in faith. As the Scripture declares, "By faith the just will obtain life."

Paul reminds the pastor and us that conversion isn't something we do; it is an act of God. While conversion certainly *includes* man making a sincere and self-conscious decision to follow Christ, it's more than that. Scripture teaches that we turn to Christ only when God supernaturally grants us spiritual life, replacing our hearts of stone with hearts of flesh. A pastor who understands conversion will have a sound philosophy of evangelism.

Evangelism is simply presenting the good news freely and trusting God to bring conversions. True faith is a supernatural gift of God, one that produces good works and prevails in holiness (*James 2:14-26*).

Pastors should certainly care about conversion. One of the most important aspects of his calling should be persuading sinners to come to repentance. He should do so from a place of peaceful confidence in God's sovereignty, not from some clever or charismatic implementation of his ingenuity. The pastor who understands that the greater result comes from putting forth God's plan, God's way will send the message that the decision to follow Christ is urgent, costly, and so worth it.

Church membership and discipleship are two significant factors that should be considered when selecting a pastor. Growth and development are huge, but so often too much focus is placed on numbers. Pastors must remember that God will not give them or send them what they can't or won't manage. Church membership and discipline set apart the people of God from the world. They will define the identity of your church. A pastor committed to church membership recognizes that he and his fellow elders are responsible for the souls of those who have covenanted themselves to their local church *(Heb. 13:17)*.

Regrettably, many pastors view church membership rolls as a way to gauge their success in ministry: the higher the numbers, the greater the sign of God's blessing. But this is misguided and grossly unbiblical. A true pastor will care not that a church's membership is large but that every individual member understands the gospel and is spiritually thriving. His primary focus won't be about growing numbers but the numbers of people growing. He will recognize that the church's membership role identifies those he is responsible for shepherding, praying for, teaching, warning, discipling, and loving.

Church discipline is taught in Scripture. That's how a church maintains the purity of its witness, guards the gospel, and warns false converts of the dangers of self-deception. Church discipline is counter-cultural and often emotionally taxing. The pastor must be both compassionate and brave enough to follow Scripture, even when it is difficult to do *(I Timothy 1:18)*. **See Footnote 5 C, Pages 103-104.**

How does the church adequately pay the pastor? The Pastor's salary is always a challenging topic in the church world. There is no single answer to this question. Every church is different, and the role of each pastor is equally unique. Both the role of the pastor and the resources to pay the pastor vary from church to church. The circumstances will determine what appropriate pay is for the pastor. The one common focus of every church should be to compensate the pastor as best as the church can afford. The manner in which the church cares for their pastor reflects the heart of its members toward God.

One very important consideration for pastors is future financial consideration. Everyone looks forward to one day being able to retire. The Pastor is no different. No one should have to work past their years of effectiveness. Too many pastors are occupying pulpits long after their effectiveness because they can't afford to retire. It is not unreasonable to structure a plan that compensates a pastor for their effectiveness in growing the church, managing the church well, equipping the saints, and preparing their successor. Several progressive-minded churches are purchasing annuities that provides for the pastor's retirement, protect his family in the event of an untimely death, and protect the church financially during a transition when a pastor decides to take a position with another church. These packages can be structured to motivate pastors to stay with a particular church. They are relatively inexpensive, but the cost of these packages increase with age. **See Footnote 5D, Page 104.**

For small churches or new church plants, paying a full-time pastor salary, plus benefits, might not work. In addition to a senior pastor, it may be impossible to hire additional pastors for specific ministries, worship leaders, etc. In these cases, it may be necessary to consider hiring a part-time or bi-vocational pastor. A bi-vocational pastor is typically someone who works another job in addition to their ministry role. In many cases, bi-vocational pastors are self-employed or work in jobs that offer flexible schedules.

In addition to paying the pastor, there are or will be other staff persons who will require financial compensation. At the inception of a start-up or new church plant, these expenditures may be more manageable than later on when the church has grown. **See the structure section and the organization chart in Footnote 1B, Pages 36-42.**

The best advice has been stated earlier in this chapter. The more effort put into the planning and forecasting phase, the clearer the picture will be regarding what qualities the church needs to finish well. Jesus said in Luke 14:28-30 –

Just imagine that you want to build a tower. Wouldn't you first sit down and estimate the cost to be sure you have enough to finish what you start? 29 If you lay the foundation but then can't afford to finish the tower, everyone will mock you: 30 "Look at that guy who started something that he couldn't finish!"

It is also better to be as transparent as possible when considering the future direction of the church. God might send a particular pastor with a heart, mind, and financial ability to progressively grow in compensation as the church's ability to increase their benefits and/or compensation grows. Churches should reevaluate all aspects of church expenses every year. This practice aids in avoiding common mistakes like increasing compensation solely because of tenure or allowing emotions to override facts. **See Chart – Footnote 5E, Pages 105-106.**

Evaluating the pastor's family structure is also beneficial when determining their salary. A pastor with minor children will likely have different needs and concerns than a seasoned pastor who either have no children or they are grown. The church may not be able to pay for private schooling and ivy-league universities, but determining what might be possible is better decided up front, rather than when those schooling decisions arrive.

Even if the church can't afford to fully pay for the schooling, a plan can be agreed upon that might provide a certain amount of assistance. If higher education is common among the other youth in the congregation, the pastor's children should not be completely deprived of that opportunity. In Chapter 6, we will consider in more detail, a variety of elements that should be evaluated as they relate to the church family.

Footnotes – 5A-5E

Footnote 5A - God loves a cheerful giver.

Paul further conveys the point that givers must transition from the Old Testament view of tithing to a heartfelt expression of their generosity; which he says reflects the believer's relationship and devotion toward God. I ask; should our giving now, be less than what was required in the Old Testament? We must understand that it's not the amount of giving that matters most. It is the sincerity and the sacrifice behind it.

Footnote 5B - God's word, God's plan, and God's purpose.

Pastors and the body of Christ must collectively put a biblically-based plan together for the church - and follow it. God's word, God's plan, and God's purpose will never fail. We just have to align ourselves with Him and stay the course. That's how we help those who have been called into pastoral leadership to be successful.

Footnote 5C – A Growing Church

Pastors must remember that God will not give them

or send them what they can't or won't manage. Church membership and discipline set apart the people of God from the world. They will define the identity of your church. A pastor committed to church membership recognizes that he and his fellow elders are responsible for the souls of those who have covenanted themselves to their local church *(Heb. 13:17)*.

Regrettably, many pastors view church membership rolls as a way to gauge their success in ministry—the higher the numbers, the greater the sign of God's blessing. But this is misguided and grossly unbiblical. A true pastor will care not that a church's membership is large but that every individual member understands the gospel and is spiritually thriving.

Footnote 5 D – Preparing for your pastor's retirement

Most annuities are designed for a 7–10 year maturity. They can be structured with renewals, additional policies, and other benefits. The church must give consideration to the age of the pastor, when he plans to retire, and what the successor plan entails. A consultation with a financial planner will provide all the necessary guidance needed to assess what the annuity structure should include what it will cost the church, and the churches affordability. There are a number of options. I am not an expert in that field, but I have seen a variety of plans that eliminated the stress that so many pastors have to deal with when they were pastoring with a no-plan, plan.

Footnote 5 E – How to determine the pastor's salary.

The Pastor's salary is always a challenging topic in the church world. There is no single answer to this question. Every church is different, and the role of each pastor is equally unique. Both the role of the pastor and the resources to pay the pastor vary from church to church.

When it comes to setting pastor salaries, there are a number of factors to consider. The size of the church and the specific ministry role are two of the most important factors. A church leadership team could be established and can collectively consider many factors, including:

- **Experience:** Pastors with more experience in ministry are typically paid more.

- **Education**: Pastors with higher levels of education are also typically paid more.

- **Role:** The pastor's specific role in the church can affect their salary.

- **Church size and attendance**: The size of the church and the number of people who attend can impact a pastor's salary.

- **Cost of living**: The cost of living in the local area should be taken into account.

- **Compensation at similar churches**: What other

churches of similar size pay their pastors can be a factor.

- **Non-church salaries**: What people with similar skills earn outside of the church can also be considered.

- **Other factors**: Other factors that can affect a pastor's salary include performance, tenure, inflation, job description, and organizational charts.

Chapter 6
The Church Family

And all those who had believed in Jesus as Savior were together and had all things in common, considering their possessions to belong to the group as a whole. Day after day they met in the temple area, continuing with one mind, and breaking bread in various private homes. They were eating their meals together with joy and generous hearts, praising God continually, and the Lord kept adding to their number daily those who were being saved.

Acts 2:44, 46-47

When God created mankind, He blessed us with the privilege of being His royal and priestly family *(I Peter 2:9)*. God's first command was to "be fruitful and multiply in number; fill the earth and subdue it" to prepare the earth for the fullness of His glory and eternal praise. God also established the family as the main social component by which this multi-generational mission would be accomplished *(Genesis 2:19–24)*. This is why, in most circumstances when a family works well, we move forward in the purposes for which God created us. When it does not, we are severely hindered in our service to Him.

God's church is expected to be a group of called-out people in relationships who do life together. Relationships are vital because the expectations of God's purpose are realized and demonstrated within those relationships. Purposeful life can be lived out when we are abiding in relationships with one another. This is where we learn to use and put into practice the Fruit of the Spirit that God has placed within us.

God calls His Church the family of God. The early church met together in the temple courts but also met together in homes where they were devoted to deep abiding relationships. They became a spiritual family. We can see many of the characteristics of a family exhibited in Acts 2:42–47.

On that day about three thousand took him at his word, were baptized, and were signed up. They committed themselves to the teaching of the apostles, the life together, the common meal, and the prayers. Everyone around was in awe of all those wonders and signs done through the apostles! And all the believers lived in a wonderful harmony, holding everything in common. They sold whatever they owned and pooled their resources so that each person's need was met. They followed a daily discipline of worship in the Temple followed by meals at home, every meal a celebration, exuberant and joyful, as they praised God. People in general liked what they saw. Every day their number grew as God added those who were saved.

The actions of these men and women not only depict the attitudes and actions of a family, they are also the kind of union and relationships that develop in a small group. A small group is a space where people can be relational while disciplining others as part of their spiritual family. **See Footnote 6A, Page 119.**

The church family includes the people in the pews around us. Much like our biological family, we haven't chosen them for ourselves, they have been chosen for us, and we are eternally connected to them. We all belong to Christ, and consequently, we are all a part of his family. In John 19:26-27, John records the account of Jesus's crucifixion.

"When Jesus saw his mother and disciple whom he loved standing nearby, he said to his mother, 'Woman, behold your son!' Then he said to the disciple, 'Behold, your mother!' And from that hour the disciple took her to his own home."

At Christ's declaration, Mary and John became family to one another and demonstrated all the loyalty we would expect from a biological mother and son. When Paul wanted the Roman church to welcome and help Phoebe, he called her "our sister" (Rom. 16:1); when Peter wanted to recognize Silvanus, he called him "a faithful brother" (1 Pet. 5:12). When the writers of the New Testament wanted to address an entire congregation, they frequently called them "brothers" or "brothers and sisters." I say again, the people in the pews around us are our family.

Throughout the New Testament, God commands us to communal care in the local church. Throughout the epistles, we are told what it means to be brothers and sisters in Christ. They also teach us "how we are to behave in the household of God" (1 Tim. 3:15). These letters remind us that life in God's family will redirect our faithfulness away from a Sunday-only concept to every hour of everyday perspective.

The church family is not a man-made family, organism, or organization. It is a God-made, selfless organism where individual preferences and priorities take a backseat to family priorities (Acts 4:32; Phil. 2:3-4). When we realize, recognize, and submit to this level of thinking, we open our hearts and our doors. We share our dinner table with those that are less fortunate. We share in the grief and disappointments of others. We compassionately add them to our prayer lists. Most importantly, we look for ways to show them the love of God.

God's people are our family. We must open our hearts and our doors to each other. There will be times when we will need to pull up another chair to the dinner table and discover that we need to add another name to our prayer list. As the family of God, we may need to share in one another's grief, trials, and disappointments. In doing so, we reflect the love of God.

Knowing this, we can delight in the particular people God has given us as brothers and sisters, no matter how unexceptional they may seem, because, in them, we apprehend something of Christ. As they grow and mature in the family circle, their character and conduct become more and more like the One our souls love best. Because of the work of His Spirit, they speak his words, love his ways, hate his enemies, reflect his holiness, and serve his ends. The more we become like Christ and the more they become like Christ, the more we will love them. This may result in added sorrow in the natural, but in the spiritual, we will experience more joy. As we build our relationship with the people of our local church and show affection for them, we demonstrate to the world that we are not ashamed to call them brothers and sisters. Within our Christian brothers and sisters, we can see something the world cannot: Christ himself.

Church leaders also have a responsibility in the development of the church family. God has given them the responsibility to serve, equip, and develop others within the church family. They are called to nourish the holistic needs of their members as well as their spiritual needs. Their agenda should include providing them with resources to properly navigate the struggles encountered in their generation. They are not tasked with changing them into what God proposes for their life. However, they should be providing opportunities for productive change. They must be willing to talk to and listen to the youth, young adults, seniors, and middle-aged members of the church family. This begins with not only asking what challenges each of those groups are facing but also by providing answers. **See footnote 6B, Page 119.**

Very few people acknowledge how long and deeply the human family has been broken. Every home has brokenness from the day it begins. When God made humanity, He blessed us with the privilege of being His royal and priestly family. God first ordained that we should "be fruitful and multiply; fill the earth and subdue it" to prepare the earth for the fullness of His glory and eternal praise. God also established the family as the main social unit by which this multi-generational mission would be fulfilled *(Gen. 2:19–24)*. It wasn't long before Adam and Eve sinned and fell under the judgment of God. God can restore families and use the tragedies that deeply hurt us to move us forward in the purposes for which He created us. He is our hope in all the brokenness we face in our lives.

When we become a part of God's family, He provides everything we need to fulfill His calling and purposes for our lives. He does this corporately to equip the church family with the tools to accomplish His directives. Sometimes, He provides these necessities directly by way of the Holy Spirit. Other times, He uses others to come alongside of us to develop and equip the saints (2 Timothy 3:16-17). In partnership, the church leadership has a responsibility to provide direction and guidance. The church must then absorb and apply those principles to their daily lives. When these principles are harmoniously applied, growth and effectiveness are realized.

In the previous chapter, we expounded on the role and responsibilities of the church leader. With those principles in mind, we must also understand that the leader's effectiveness is predicated on the follower's level of commitment. The following phrase illustrates the expected trajectory of the church family – individually and collectively.

The first stage in a believer's walk should be the discovery phase. God's desire for each of us is stated in two passages; Luke 10:27 and Matthew 28:18-20.

Love the Lord your God with all your heart, with all your soul, with all your strength, and with all your mind; and your neighbor as yourself.

Go therefore and make disciples of all the nations. Help the people to learn of Me, believe in Me, and obey My words, baptizing them in the name of the Father and of the Son and of the Holy Spirit, teaching them to observe everything that I have commanded you; and lo, I am with you always. I will remain with you perpetually, regardless of circumstance, and on every occasion, even to the end of the age.

God wants us to go wherever He plants or sends us with a mindset to make disciples. He wants us to baptize them, teach them, and assure them that He will be with them at all times. To that end, we must establish and develop a relationship with Him. That is the discovery stage. During that stage, we begin to understand who God is, what He expects from us, and how instrumental He is in orchestrating our development and relationship with Him. It's vitally important that we stay engaged in that relationship before we venture into community ministry. Once we have effectively fulfilled our time with Him in the discovery stage, we can effectively engage with others in the ministry for whom He has called us. **See Footnote 6C, Page 120.**

After we discover what our calling and purpose are, we must also realize that God will provide others on our journey to assist in our development. This stage is called discipleship. Discipleship, apprenticeship, and mentoring are all about developing Godly character for the mission He assigns. It could be one person, or a number of people, but either way, God will put people in your life to demonstrate and develop what is needed to fulfill what He has asked of us. It is important to remember that discipleship is a continuous process. **See Footnote 6D, Page 120.**

Once we progress from discovery and discipleship, we need direction. The direction seems simple, but so often, it becomes more complicated than we expected. Andy Stanley wrote a book titled, *The Principle of the Path*. The thesis of the book is that direction determines destiny, not desire. He points out that no matter how much we desire to reach a particular place in life, if our direction is not aligned with it, we won't get there.

When we have a good understanding of what God wants from us and we have been effectively discipled/mentored, we only need to aim our lives in the direction that supports that objective. God will bring it to fruition *(Isaiah 55:11)*. **See Footnote 6E, Page 120.**

So shall my word be that goes forth out of my mouth: it shall not return unto me void, but it shall accomplish that which I please, and it shall prosper in the thing whereto I sent it.

The last ingredient in our quest for success is discipline. Discipline should be utilized in all four stages. Discipline is not only applying a set of rules and principles to our behavior, but also obeying them. It can and should be used in all aspects of our Christian walk. In every area of life, discipline, or the lack of it, usually shows. For believers, it will guide us in our civil and moral decisions. **See Footnote 6F, Pages 120-121.**

Our focus thus far has been on the spiritual aspects of the church family. From a holistic perspective, other elements of family development must be addressed. The church family has some factors beyond the spiritual that need to be developed as well. The church family is comprised of men, women, and children of various ages. God has expectations of each. Men may be single or married, and they may also have children. Whatever the demographic, men are expected to work, provide, protect, teach, and nurture themselves, their wife, and their children.

Women are expected to care for their husbands, themselves, their children, and the home. Children have a responsibility to obey their parents. The word of God supports these endeavors.

To those who are unmarried or widowed, here's my advice: it is a good thing to stay single as I do. If they do not have self-control, they should go ahead and get married. It is much better to marry than to be obsessed by sexual urges.

I Cor. 7:8-9

Husbands, love your wives, even as Christ also loved the church, and gave himself for it;

Eph. 5:25

Wives, submit yourselves unto your own husbands, as unto the Lord.

Eph. 5:22

Children obey your parents in the Lord: for this is right (Eph. 6:1). Fathers, do not provoke your children to wrath: but bring them up in the nurture and admonition of the Lord (Eph. 6:4).

With those instructions in mind, the church family must assist families in developing the social skills, and in some instances, technical skills to find meaningful and productive employment. The church family has the primary responsibility in supporting the church building and the administrative costs associated with its functionality. **See Footnote 6G, Page 121.**

As I mentioned in the introduction *(in the last paragraph of page 12),* the church should be the most reliable and trustworthy institution in providing a meaningful vocation that aligns itself with the morality and civility that the church represents. God provides everything the church family needs to accomplish His calling for each family He establishes. The challenge for the church is to identify who has the potential to develop and provide those collective needs to complete the assignment given to them.

Discipleship is one of the ways this can be achieved. In many instances, there are professional members of the family who can tutor younger individuals (and even others who may not be necessarily younger) in developing multiple people who possess the skills necessary to provide the talent needed to support the church.

If a particular skill set is lacking, in-service training from outside sources can be brought in to develop what's needed. Either way, the church has a responsibility to utilize every opportunity available to equip the saints for sustaining the families God entrusts to them and acknowledging the work of the gospel.

And He personally gave some to be apostles, some prophets, some evangelists, some pastors and teachers, for the training of the saints in the work of ministry, to build up the body of Christ, until we all reach unity in the faith and in the knowledge of God's Son, growing into a mature man with a stature measured by Christ's fullness. Eph. 4:11-13

Every church family should have an education and training department. Every church should have a mission statement and goals that align with it. After members answer the questionnaire that focuses on the mission statement and their skills, their responses will aid in revealing the church's specific training and development needs. If there are members who can provide those resources, they should be the best to serve in those areas.

In areas where those resources are not in-house, partnering with other churches that have those resources is a great option. After all, the church (*local and global*) is collectively one church - the body of Christ. If neither option is available to the church, reaching out to institutions that can provide that service might be the best option. This will become the more costly option, but failing to do any of these will weaken the church and limit its effectiveness in those areas. **See Footnote 6H, Page 122.**

In Chapter 7, we will take a closer look at what effective education and training look like.

Footnotes-6A-6H

Footnote 6A – Discipling through small groups.

If the members of your church are truly a part of God's family (*saved*), they are an eternal part of your family. Not only will we have these people in our lives on this side, but they will also be with us in our heavenly home.

People grow and develop like crops planted in a field. They may not look like much to us, but that doesn't mean they are not a part of His family. God may be growing them in ways that we can't see. Our responsibility is to plant and water; if growth occurs, God causes that to happen *(I Cor. 3:6)*. We might as well learn how to see and treat them as brothers and sisters now. More importantly, that's what God expects us to do during our time on earth.

Footnote 6B – Opportunity for change.

Ask your church family (all demographics) to complete a survey, and encourage honesty. Develop a committee that will process the data. Through research and proven models, put a list of ideas together that best address their concerns and revisit their responses with a plan of implementing solutions to their concerns.

Footnote 6C – Discovering our calling and purpose.

Our calling and purpose are not what we have to find. God has not hidden them from us. We must discover what they are, and God aids us in that quest. He will reveal it but, it is a process (*Isaiah 28:13*).

Footnote 6D – Discipleship.

Some examples of discipleship, mentoring, and assistance are – Moses and Aaron, Eli and Samuel, David and Johnathan, Paul and Timothy, Paul, and Titus, and most pointedly, Jesus and His disciples.

Footnote 6E– Direction.

God does not say that we won't encounter opposition and challenges or sometimes move in the wrong direction. What He does say is that He is greater than our mistakes and He will use our mistakes to strengthen and guide us to His desired end (Romans 8:28).

Footnote 6F– Discipline.

Discipline requires work. The very nature of discipline seems to focus on addressing areas of our life that is unbridled and usually produce unwanted results. The lack of discipline often shows itself in dieters over-eating, financial troubles from overspending, injuries from over-exercising, fatigue from overworking, and weak/immature Christians from inconsistent or lack of study. Balance is probably the optimal mission. Developing discipline equips us with the stick-to-it-ness needed to be successful and effective.

Footnote 6G– Delegation of responsibilities.

So often, church members believe they initiated and decided the church for which they would be a part. What we sometimes fail to realize is that it is God who has orchestrated our path (Prov. 3:5). We might ask, why here? Throughout our lives, God has been imputing skills along our journey in preparation for assisting in the church operation in some way or another.

If you have administrative skills, you should offer them to the church family. If you have technical skills, you should be using them for the advancement of the church. If you have professional skills, you should be sharing that area of expertise with the church family. It could be that God has sent you to a certain congregation to eliminate the need for that church to pay for that service. Even if it has to be paid for, the cost should be less and the confidence in the work should be greater.

Footnote 6H – Educate, Demonstrate, and Elevate.

In *Mark 1:17, Jesus said unto His disciples, Come ye after me, and I will make you to become fishers of men.* God's plan has always been to elevate people through training and demonstration. It worked for Him, and it will certainly work for us. So much of what we live by and learn from is a result of the education and demonstration He provided to the disciples. Of course, we are empowered by the Holy Spirit, but as Jesus reminded them –

But the Comforter, which is the Holy Spirit, whom the Father will send in my name, he shall teach you all things, and bring all things to your remembrance, whatsoever I have said unto you.

John 14:26

Chapter 7
Education & Training

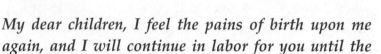

My dear children, I feel the pains of birth upon me again, and I will continue in labor for you until the Anointed One is formed completely in you.

Galatians 4:19

Throughout scripture, the significance of education and training is illustrated. In Acts 7:22, we read that *Moses was learned in all wisdom of the Egyptians, and was mighty in words and deeds.* In Exodus 18:20, the word of God says, *you shall teach them ordinances and laws, and shall shew them the way wherein they must walk, and the work that they must do.* In II Timothy 3:14-16, Paul writes, *But continue thou in the things which thou hast learned and hast been assured of, knowing of whom thou hast learned them; And that from a child thou hast known the holy scriptures, which can make thee wise unto salvation through faith which is in Christ Jesus. All scripture is given by inspiration of God, and is profitable for doctrine, for reproof, for correction, for instruction in righteousness.* He further states above that his labor would continue until Christ completely forms in them. These are just a few passages throughout Scripture that encourage knowledge, education, and training in righteousness. **See Footnote 7A, Page 134.**

The importance of education is seen in the secular

environment. What's not as evident is the substantive benefit of expanded learning for the church. God categorizes this appetite for learning with wisdom. In Proverbs 4:7, we read, *Wisdom is the principal thing; therefore get wisdom: and with all thy getting, get understanding.* God does not oppose secular learning. Most of the world's working class has honed their skills through secular education. What God desires is that we pursue every aspect of our lives from a foundational perspective that's supported by biblical wisdom, knowledge, principles, and standards.

Many practices used in leading and managing secular organizations are also used to organize and manage the church. The difference is often revealed in the moral character and integrity of those leading. I am certainly not saying that all church leaders lead with character and integrity and all secular leaders lead without those traits. However, I do believe that those who are committed to Godly principles will more often lead with character and integrity.

In Genesis 3, we are provided the details of how mankind (*Adam and Eve*) traded innocence for a sinful nature. In Chapter 4, we see sin revealing its tragic nature through the fatal act of Cain. Over the centuries since then, the depravity of man has progressed and intensified. All of us have descended from that sinful nature. Even those within the church family came out of the world into the church. It is Christian education and training, and the grace of God that enables them to exhibit Christian character in their daily lives.

Today, education and training, both Christian and secular, are critical to the church's success. The challenges and dynamics associated with families today are much more complicated than in years past. Generations passed, and many church leaders, like a number of secular organizations, were successfully led and operated by leaders with very little (*if any*) management-level education. In years past, leaders made head or heart decisions. When they were right, it was a hallelujah moment. When they were wrong, they implemented a recovery plan. Most of those businesses survived and some even thrived.

As stated in the introduction section of this book (*page 8, second paragraph*), Jesus didn't come to build institutions, He came to build people because the people of God become the church of God. We see that modeled in His life and throughout His ministry. He devoted the ministry portion of His life to investing in individuals. That's what each of us who are followers of Christ should be doing. The programs, titles, buildings, and all the shiny objects that we deem holy and sacred in American culture and around the world are not what the Bible calls holy.

George Barna, a leading expert in church and worldview trends said, "*People have become more selfish, churches have become less influential, pastors have become less Bible-centric. Families have invested less of their time and energy in spiritual growth, particularly of their children. The media now influences the Church more than the Church influences the media, or the culture for that matter. The Christian Body tends to get off track arguing about a lot of things that don't matter."*

Building and developing people biblically and holistically requires an honest assessment of at least two truths. One of them is the fact that every leader will one day need to step aside and embrace new leadership. Secondly, if the church is to continue to grow productively, biblically, and with relevance, future leaders must be mentored and prepared for the job. That preparation should begin on day one, not 6 months – a year before a change in leadership occurs.

One of the most troubling trends Barna highlights is the decline in discipleship and a lack of solid, biblical training from seminaries. He criticized the prevalent metrics used by churches to gauge success. Too often the focus is placed on attendance, fundraising, and infrastructure. Enormous effort was placed on the functionality of things that have little to do with Jesus's mission.

Barna also stated that while many seminaries have "good intentions," they set young ministry leaders up for failure. "There is poor leadership in seminaries that mislead local churches into thinking that they're training individuals whom God has called to be leaders. What they fail to realize is "You get what you measure. If you measure the wrong things, you'll get the wrong outcomes." Too often, pastors measure success and effectiveness by how many people show up, how much money they raise, how many programs they offer, how many staff persons they hire, and how much square footage they build out. If these are the metrics you're tracking, you're measuring the wrong factors, and consequently, you're getting the wrong outcomes. Jesus didn't die for any of that.

Rather than fixating on buildings and programs, churches must turn their focus on children. The children are not only our future but also our present. Through focused education and training, we can prepare them for optimal outcomes. The biblical vision for educating children involves teaching them God's Word, God's laws, God's works, and God's character.

Then you will grasp what it means to truly respect the Eternal God, and you will have discovered the knowledge of the one True God.

Proverbs 2:5

Parents have the primary responsibility to raise their children to become spiritually equipped. They often believe they can produce the necessary learning by teaching children scripture on weekends. Reinforcing learning on weekends is certainly beneficial, but local churches need to support parents in that endeavor. The Bible reminds us – *When there is no vision, the people will perish"* (*Prov. 29:18*). Collectively, a joint focus needs to be on the children and growing their biblical vision and worldview. **See**

Footnote 7B, Page 135.

Since parents have the responsibility to nurture their children in education and training, they must equip themselves in that area as well. Until the youth are prepared to take on leadership roles in the church, parents must serve as demonstrators, facilitators, tutors, and mentors. Utilizing the knowledge and skills possessed by adult leadership is just the first step. The skills needed that are not present in the church warrant a search for those skills in other arenas. Where do you find them?

Other churches may be able to assist, but there are also options in different non-profit organizations. Potential candidates can attend non-profit conferences that offer courses that will provide information to equip members with the skills to perform human resource responsibilities.

There are building maintenance training programs available that will assist with delivering skills to maintain your church building. These are areas where youth can be incorporated into learning the importance of performing and executing those maintenance functions. Every function performed by in-house labor reduces costs and funds that otherwise would have to be paid to outside sources. These endeavors will often identify potential candidates who might possess the innate interest to later pursue a life career in the technical skills area. **See Footnote 7C, Page 135.**

As leaders within the church, we must assist those in the Body of Christ to develop a better understanding and insight into what they believe, why they believe it, and how these beliefs translate into their future actions. The collective empowerment of parents and church leaders with spiritual and secular empowerment of its youth produces intentional disciplining of future generations. In a civics class during my high school years, I read a quote that said, *"A society is best known by how it treats its youth, it's most vulnerable, and the elderly."* I believe the Bible supports that quote.

Jesus said to the disciples, Let the children come to Me, and don't ever stand in their way, for this is what the kingdom of God is all about.

Mark 10:14

Say no to wrong. Learn to do good. Work for justice. Help the down-and-out. Stand up for the homeless. Go to bat for the defenseless.

Isaiah 1:17

Then shall Jesus answer them, saying, "Truly I say unto you, since ye did it not to one of the least of these, ye did it not to me."

Matthew 25:45

Religion that is pure and undefiled before God the Father is this: to visit orphans and widows in their affliction and to keep ourselves unstained from the world.

James 1:27

In fairness, I believe the majority of the workload should be supplied by the middle-aged group. Generally, they can exert more energy because they are also more resilient. We teach the youth while they are young, but we should do this with love and compassion. Their youth should be the most enjoyable time of their lives. I spoil the elderly. I think they should be rewarded for all of the sacrifices and hard work they've given in paving the way for those coming behind them. The vulnerable can also benefit from our help, assistance, and compassion. Whatever we can do to make life more palatable for them, we should do it, if we can. If not for the grace of God, we could be in a similar situation.

I like this model because it provides an opportunity for all of us to enjoy our youth and elder years. This view may not be shared by all, but that is where education and training opportunities can be fruitful. I remember my first job as a laborer. I was a part of a seven-man team. Five of the seven were 49-72 years of age. My partner and I were 28 and 19, respectively. We were always given more physical jobs. I didn't understand it then, and I didn't agree with it. Now, much older and wiser, I fully understand it and agree with that concept.

A good work ethic can take you a long way. Even hard work has benefits. God gave man a work assignment when He created him and placed him in the Garden of Eden.

The Lord God took the man and put him in the Garden of Eden to till it and keep it.

Gen. 2:15

Physical work is not appealing to everyone. Some are more inclined to pursue academic or technical work. The world is large enough to accommodate all three endeavors. Many of our technological advancements have come about because someone was motivated to find an easier or more efficient way to accomplish a task. **See Footnote 7D, Page 135.**

As Paul stated in II Thessalonians 3:10,

For even when we were with you, we gave you this command: If anyone will not work, let him not eat.

I'm not suggesting that we need to adopt a pay-to-play mentality. I'm just saying that work is a healthy endeavor, the Word of God supports it, and when we give considerable thought to what type of work best suits us, work can be a productive experience for our families and our church family. When we expand our perspective on education and training beyond the church pews, there are a plethora of holistic benefits we can realize.

We currently have an obesity crisis within our society, inside and outside of the church. Too often, church events provide food choices that are not in the best interest of its members. If we are going to promote healthy living (spiritual and physical), we must avoid the hypocrisy trap where too many churches find themselves involved. Gatherings for fellowship that include eating are great. What diminishes its effectiveness is contributing to the obesity crisis by preparing meals that are not beneficial to the health and well-being of the church.

Physical exercise ministries are perhaps as important to the well-being of the church as their spiritual counterpart. Our physical health is what enables us to fulfill the spiritual ministries of the church. Some health challenges are genetic or may have developed over time or from aging. Unfortunately, I have seen so many street ministries reduced to almost a telemarketing outreach because people could not walk very long, climb steps, or they experienced respiratory issues from breathing problems. A physical exercise ministry may not have prevented these obstacles; however, it wouldn't have hurt the ministry either.

Financial stewardship is vitally important for the entire church. Certainly, those responsible for the financial management of the church need to be financially competent. When good money management practices are taught and used throughout the church family, the church as a whole can benefit from it, and families within the church can better manage their money. Not only does tithing become more obtainable, but other important needs in financial areas are also enhanced. Some of those areas include budgeting, savings accounts, investments, making a plan for college tuition assistance, travel, life, home, and auto insurance policies, and burial plans. **See Footnote 7E, Pages 136-138**

Investment clubs are becoming more common in churches today. Members are being taught how the financial markets operate. In addition, they are being exposed to various companies that may not be in the best interest of church investments. Some companies are producing great returns, but their products are often counterproductive to the morals and standards that the church supports. **See Footnote 7F, Page 138.**

Life skills are another matter that education and training can impact positively. As the church prepares, promotes, and presents its biblically based life-skills training, it must understand that sometimes it's being presented to individuals whose current life-skills were developed from a holistic model. We will discuss this concern in greater depth in the next chapter. **See Footnote 7G, Pages 138.**

Footnotes – 7A-7G

Footnote 7A – Biblical support for education and training.

If you search the Hebrew scripture, you will find over 350 references of words used that imply the idea of learning, teaching, education, and training. I have listed some passages from Hebrew and Greek scriptures below.

- I Tim. 6:20-21
- Prov. 1:7
- II Cor. 10:4-5
- Deut. 6:7
- Deut. 11:9
- Psalm 145:4
- II Tim. 3:15-16
- Psalm 78:5-6
- Psalm 34:11
- Eph. 6:4
- Rom. 12:1-2

Footnote 7B – Biblical education.

The objective of biblical education is to inform children and other potential learners of how to think, how to process their thoughts, support their ideas, etc. What it should not focus on is teaching them what to think. The Holy Spirit will perform that work if we provide them with the truth of God's Word.

Footnote 7C – Skilled labor education

As important as an academic education is, an academic education and training vocation may not be the calling for every child. It is much better to discover this before amassing huge tuition debt. Remember, Jesus was a carpenter, Paul was a tentmaker, and many of the disciples were fishermen. Confucius said that if you choose a job you love, you don't have to work a day in your life.

Footnote 7D – Technological Advancements

Thomas Edison created the first metal filament in 1878 and turned it into the first commercially viable light bulb. Cell phones changed the world. Seventy-five percent of the people on Earth have a mobile phone. Eli Whitney invented the cotton gin which separated cotton from cotton seeds. Manufacturers use robots to perform repetitious tasks that increase efficiency and proficiency.

Footnote 7E – Financial Stewardship

Budgeting - The term "budgeting" often produces a sense of restraint. Referring to it as a money management plan might make it more palatable. I suggest a 10-10-80 method. Give 10% to God's work, 10% for investments, and 80% on my living arrangements. Whether it's my plan or another plan, there needs to be a disciplined financial plan. Otherwise, financial issues will often show up as a surprise expense.

Checking & Savings Accounts – Checking and Savings accounts offer a variety of benefits. There are different requirements for various benefits. Some account types offer higher percentage yields, free checks, minimum balance requirements, and other features to help decide what works best for you.

Investments – Investments are not just risky money thrown at the stock market. 401K plans through employers is a good investing option. CDs are good and safe options. Investing in Real Estate is a little more aggressive, yet a safe option. The stock market risk can be reduced by selecting a group of minimum to low-level mutual funds.

College Tuition - Making a plan for college tuition might include your 401K or a designated college savings plan. Any of the suggestions mentioned above could be used as a college savings plan. If the potential college student has a technical interest, an apprenticeship can be completed in 3-4 years, and they pay very well. In addition, many of them will pay for, or reimburse college tuition.

Travel – Travel is often decided based on the funds available. People are now creating travel groups. They collectively choose places to travel, have a group of travelers they know, and the cost is usually reduced because of the greater numbers of travelers.

Insurance - Whether Auto, Home, or Life Insurance, we need to do a better job of securing these resources. Basic auto insurance protects you from lawsuits and financial devastation. Homeowners Insurance, even if it has a high deductible, protects the homeowner from frivolous lawsuits and major losses when there is no coverage at all. These insurances should be reviewed at least bi-annually in search for a better and more affordable plan.

Burial – Most cemeteries offer a basic burial insurance plan that could at a minimum, eliminate families from engaging in *GoFundMe* options. These challenging times can be most embarrassing for families during what may be their most vulnerable times in life. Lastly, including your church in your estate planning is always a worthwhile endeavor for those that may not have surviving family members, or may have a desire to leave a legacy that others will benefit from for generations.

Bankers, financial planners, and other nonprofit

organizations will provide more in-depth information with these services at no cost.

Footnote 7F – Investment Options

Members of a church are no different than any other member of society as it relates to what they can legally invest in. Where they differ, or should differ is what investments they choose. I've held discussions with several potential investors who wrestled with the prospect of investing in Hemp (cannabis or marijuana). I'm told the return on investment is lucrative. The medical association argues that it offers benefits in pain management and pain reduction. It's believed that it also aids in increasing patient's appetites. Some law enforcement jurisdictions believe it impairs judgment, reflexes, and decision-making. Several states have legalized its use, but the debate continues.

Footnote 7G– Life-Skills

The church, more so than any other institution, must always remember that the "church family" is comprised of people from every culture, economic level, family dynamic, and religious or non-religious persuasion. It is through our love, empathy, patience, and mentoring that we provide each member of the family an opportunity to grow, develop, and one day accept us as we accept them for who they are.

Chapter 8
Social *and* Political
Responsibilities

A Samaritan traveling the road came upon a man that had been attacked. When he saw the man's condition, his heart went out to him. He gave him first aid, disinfecting and bandaging his wounds. Then he lifted him onto his donkey, led him to an inn, and made him comfortable. In the morning he took out two silver coins and gave them to the innkeeper, saying, 'Take good care of him. If it costs any more, put it on my bill. I'll pay you on my way back.'

Luke 10:33-35

In the early church, there was always a connection between doctrine and action. This connection reflected the apostles' teachings, which they obtained from Jesus. Jesus was committed to a holistic ministry. He didn't just perform good works, He did so while preaching and teaching the good news of the gospel. If the church is going to follow and fulfill the teachings of Jesus, we too will have to address the root of mankind's problems and apply the teachings of Christ.

Social Responsibilities

When Jesus told the story about the Samaritan, His purpose was to show that no one, regardless of race, creed, or culture was beyond the reach of God. He also revealed through this story how God uses all situations to demonstrate the power of God to change lives. He revealed how a perceived outsider can be used to show others how to be a real neighbor and respond to a crisis. If the church is going to be successful and effective, these practices must be modeled. The methods used may differ, but the message and ministry objectives must remain the same.

The unique opportunity that social justice provides to the church is not only that Jesus modeled it, but also that it is an activity that is to be modeled by the church and individually. As part of the Body of Christ, we can individually demonstrate social justice, and in many instances, more effectively as a group. Our activity will often affect one or more people who are either struggling or ignorant of the gospel of Jesus Christ.

As a group, we can make a greater impact on systems, organizations, institutions, and most importantly, other churches and their impact on the kingdom. Our primary obligation is to share the good news of Jesus Christ with a dying world that may not be aware that God offers a gift of salvation to anyone who will accept it. In addition, God expects us to show that same kind of love and compassion in our lives and activities.

For this is the message that ye heard from the beginning, that we should love one another.

My little children let us not love in word, neither in tongue; but in deed and in truth.

I John 3:11 & 18

Jesus did not come into our sphere to be served, but to serve. The purpose of the church is not that it might be served, but would become a servant or of service to the world. Christ calls believers to be His disciples. He wants us to give our entire being.

I beseech you therefore, brethren, by the mercies of God, that ye present your bodies a living sacrifice, holy, acceptable unto God, which is your reasonable service. And be not conformed to this world: but be ye transformed by the renewing of your mind, that ye may prove what is that good, and acceptable, and perfect, will of God.

Romans 12:1-2

We are expected to live as strangers in this world for the sake of the world. As the Body of Christ, we look forward to a new world in which all social injustice, politics, and cultural challenges have been brought under the merciful and just reign of Christ.

The church must stand for Christian principles and speak out against social disorder when the world's order contradicts it. It is the duty of believers, as citizens to reshape disorder and conform to God's principles. This should not be done in any unlawful or forceful manner. A successful and sustainable change must be done in the spirit of Christ and by Christian principles.

> *"Injustice anywhere is a threat to justice everywhere."*
> *Dr. Martin Luther King Jr.*

He wrote this in a letter from jail in 1963, explaining that all communities and states are connected and that what affects one directly affects all. His quote on social injustice implies that if any part of our country lacks equality, it threatens progress toward equality for the entire country. The church is not just the local assembly that you or I attend. It includes all assemblies that truly stand on the Christian principles of Jesus Christ. **See Footnote 8A, Pages 155-156.**

Historical data indicates that racial disparity has been and continues to be problematic in our society. In 2020, Barna conducted a study on race relations. The study revealed that –

Social media has twisted and spiraled with resources and hashtags. Books on anti-racism have risen to best-seller lists. Leaders in government, business, and religious institutions have requested public examination of the actions and influence of social media.

In 2020, COVID-19 not only introduced a medical pandemic, it also created social media crises. For decades, church leaders pushed the message that churches, families, and the Christian world are strengthened because of the personal interaction, experienced through physical fellowship. As fellow parishioners rub elbows and share their stories, struggles, and victories, others gain strength and increased faith. The writer of Hebrews reinforces that position when he says,

Let us consider thoughtfully how we may encourage one another to love and to do good deeds, not forsaking our meeting together as believers for worship and instruction, as is the habit of some, but encouraging one another, and all the more faithfully as you see the day of Christ's return] approaching.

Hebrews 10:24-25

During COVID-19, the *Director of the National Institute of Allergy and Infectious Disease* discouraged social gatherings. Several churches pivoted to online streaming. It was different; it required some adjustments and created some technical challenges for non-tech-savvy members. There were growing pains, but after balancing it all, many became quite fond of it. One observation that was quickly exposed was in the financial giving. There were several giving apps available if you knew how to use them. The USPS was an option, you could hand deliver to a drop box, or you could do as so many did, STOP GIVING.

Some churches were not set up for streaming. Many of them could not afford streaming equipment. They seemed to be left with one of two options: meet in person against the advice of the NIAID, or close the doors. I don't have the statistical data, but I know some churches continued to meet in person and a small number experienced great tragedy. I also know of some churches that closed their doors and some of them have not reopened.

The last group I want to address is people who have become too comfortable with streaming. They often referred to it as, going to church in their pajamas, eating breakfast while worshipping, bedside Baptist, and probably several other references you may have heard. Some of them faithfully sent in their giving, but many did not. A phrase that was commonly shared with me was, *"I guess you can be a part of a church without physically being there?"*

So, allow me to condense this. Hebrews 10:24-25

did not say that we lose our salvation if we forsake gathering all together. It says that when we do, we tend to lose our way, our values, our principles, and in some ways, our minds. COVID-19 presented a God-allowed challenge. During the recovery period, some were comfortable with what they had become. Many became isolated from their best support. **See Footnote 8B, Page 156.**

The thief comes only to steal and to kill and to destroy.

John 10:10

The thief that Jesus is referring to is Satan. His mission in all of his efforts is to do just what Jesus said. He, however, does not want to take away your existence. He desires to take away your effectiveness. Just like he did in the garden, he wants us to stay around and do his bidding to destroy our productive effectiveness. God said in *Genesis 2:17*- **But of the tree of the knowledge of good and evil, thou shalt not eat of it: for in the day that you eat of it, you shall surely die.** Satan said to Eve in *Genesis 3:4* - **You shall not surely die.** Adam and Eve did not die physically, but they lost the perfect effective position they held before sinning.

Satan wants to *steal* your joy. He wants to *kill* your testimony. He wants to *destroy* your effectiveness. How does he do that? He does it through isolation from the fellowship and relationship with God and God's people. That's what he did through COVID-19, and that's what he's doing to so many through social media. So much attention has been given to Facebook, Twitter, Instagram, TikTok, Snapchat, and others.

Too many people (*non-Christians and Christians*) have become so focused on social friends, likes, views, and followers of people who are uninformed and people they may never know. Our efforts would be better utilized pursuing what God likes. Social media has tremendous benefits when used properly. The word of God reaches so many across the world through social media. Education and training in so many areas of learning are shared through social media. Families are now using mediums like Zoom to connect with family members regularly. Before Zoom, it might have been years before they could see each other. That being said, social media should not replace personal engagement; it should be used to enhance it. We only addressed the first part of *John 10:10*. Jesus said in the b portion of verse 10 -

But I have come so that you may have life and have it in abundance.

Barna also stated that even *within the church, there seems to be a sense that people are doubling down on division.* When we consider the segregation of races as it relates to Sunday morning worship services, these results are not surprising. Until there is a more concerted effort made to socialize with other believers who don't particularly look like us, it's unlikely that differing cultures will come to realize that we have much more in common than uncommon.

It is not unusual to hear various church groups referred to as – *a black church or a white church*. Do Christians believe that there will be racial separation in the kingdom? Do they think that only one race will enter God's kingdom? Does any race that believes that believe their race is the chosen race? Do Christians not know that with God, there is only one race – the human race? What is it that causes God's people to think that once we're in heaven, we'll then become the well-adjusted and well-accepting people of God? God has called us to be all of that now. That's what we're supposed to be developing in this life.

In team sports, players are expected to be good sports and accept a loss. When players have difficulty grasping that idea, they can end up on the bench. Only one team can be awarded the title of winner. Unfortunately, poor sportsmanship and refusal to admit losing or wrongdoing are becoming too common in other competitive areas of life. When corrupt behavior migrates into the church, it must be addressed and confronted. When it's not, principles are weakened, apathy may develop, and the church will look no different than the world. **See Footnote 8C, Pages 156-157.**

In 1 Corinthians 5:1-5, Paul addressed lewd or unchristian-like behavior in the Corinthian church. He was beside himself because no one seemed to be bothered by it. These kinds of behaviors must be addressed. If not, we will begin to see an infestation. Maybe we already are. I am troubled by terms that are so commonly uttered, such as **my truth** (*the way I see it*), **the greater good** (*whatever works out better in the end*), and **my bad** (*not my fault or I'm not sorry*). No one wants to take responsibility for anything!

We are fallible human beings. We will make mistakes. We will offend people, unintentionally and sometimes intentional, but there is a proper and productive way to fix these infractions: God's biblical way! God's way is not denying it; it's acknowledging it, accepting responsibility, and asking God for forgiveness. We must also ask for forgiveness from those who are offended by us.

In 1 John 1:8-10, the bible says,

If we claim that we're free of sin, we're only fooling ourselves. A claim like that is errant nonsense. On the other hand, if we admit our sins and simply come clean about them, He won't let us down; He'll be true to himself. He'll forgive our sins and purge us of all wrongdoing.

That restores our relationship with our heavenly Father. We also need to repair our fellowship with our brothers and sisters. In Matthew 18:15, we are told –

If your brother sins against you, go and admonish him in private. If he listens to you, you have won your brother.

Political Responsibilities

The separation of church and state is a political and legal concept that defines the relationship between the government and religious organizations. At its core, it is a concept in the United States based on the First Amendment of the Constitution: The first clause of the Bill of Rights states that *"Congress shall make no law respecting an establishment of religion." This means that the government can't establish a religion, favor one religion over another, or interfere with the free practice of religion."*

The church is a voluntary unincorporated association of God's people who make up its congregation. It is separated from whatever incorporated entities and trust structures it uses to operate its secular business, such as banking, property acquisitions, and other similar activities. This gives churches the freedom to have their constitution as it relates to governing their spiritual life within the assembly. Church leaders are still held accountable to governmental laws, such as taxes, labor laws, and crimes. It just means that churches can manage their internal processes according to their choosing.

The world Jesus commissions the church to reach *(Matthew 28:18-20)* with the good news is often seen running away from us, not because they reject the claims of Jesus. Too often it is because they can't tolerate the politics and hypocrisy of those who profess to be followers of Him. That doesn't mean that Christians should not have a political view or remain silent and avoid all political discussions. It means that we should compassionately and discernably choose when to have those conversations. Avoiding all political discourse and engagement is quietly supporting the status quo.

History tells us that in the early 1900s *(if that information has not been removed from history books)*, many of the slave owners were Christians; at least they attended church services. Slave ownership was big business and grossly profitable. For those reasons and perhaps others, those churches did not speak out against slavery and did not engage in political discussions about it. If they did, it was amongst other slave owners. Maybe they didn't realize that not speaking out against it or engaging in political discussion was supporting slavery.

Speaking out against injustice is not a new concept for followers of Christ. In Exodus 2:11, we see an example of this with Moses that caused him much anger. He saw an Egyptian "beating a Hebrew." This was more than slavery, but an instance of violence or perhaps even torture. Moses identified with the man who was being beaten as "one of his people." Moses realized this could have been his life if he had not been raised in Pharaoh's family.

Verse 12 says, *He looked all around and seeing no one, he struck the Egyptian dead and hid him in the sand.* I'm not advocating or excusing murder, I'm simply showing one example of political injustice and the response to it by a man of God. Even inaction is an action. Avoidance is an expression of irrelevance.

Our political involvement should be triggered by injustice of any kind, regardless of race, gender, or political affiliation. Our political positions should be established based upon God's Word, His position on it, and healthy discussion with other believers who provide wise counsel. If I only socialize with people who agree with me on everything, it will grossly affect my ability to know, love, and value people who are different. If my version of the gospel does not include loving my enemies, it's not the gospel Jesus teaches. What Christians can't continue to do is establish our beliefs and understanding based on emotions, feelings, or other beliefs that are not truthful or scripturally supported.

Exalt Him as Lord in your heart. Always be ready to offer a defense, humbly and respectfully, when someone asks why you live in hope. Keep your conscience clear so that those who ridicule your good conduct in the Anointed and say bad things about you will be put to shame.

I Peter 3:15-16

The most significant problem today with Christians and politics is not political apathy; it is the over-consumption and obsession with political matters. Our identity in Christ changes how we see everything and everyone; at least it is supposed to. If the gospel we preach is not powerful enough to break down the dividing walls of hostility between Republican Christians and Democratic Christians, is it the gospel?

If Christians become as excited about the mission of Christ as they are about their politics, we would have a revival. When someone comes through the doors of our churches, they're not seeking a position on political issues; they want to know where they stand with Christ. They need Jesus. He is the only source of healing and hope for the people of this country.

As believers in God, we have a great deal of influence on politics. Our position should introduce a deeper commitment to justice and compassion. While Christians do need to be involved in politics, they need to stay focused on a God who deeply cares about his world and his creation. The Bible is political and much of it is about how God wants His people to act towards him and towards each other. Too often, it is injustice that infects God's world, and this grieves Him. Paul says in I Timothy 2:1 –

I urge you, first of all, that requests, prayers, intercession, and thanksgiving be made for everyone, for kings and those in authority that we may live peaceful and quiet lives in all godliness and holiness. This is good and pleasing to our God and Savior. He wants all men to come to the knowledge of truth.

God wants us to understand that the government doesn't have the power to change the world. The government's responsibility is to maintain order. It is believers who have the power to make a difference. That difference will be made through the power of the Holy Spirit.

Pastors must be careful, talking about politics in the pulpit. Nowhere in scripture are people told whom to vote for. That's not just true for pastors; lay people shouldn't be telling people whom to vote for either. While Christians push their political perspectives, they may be increasing the number of dissenters of two groups; the none's, and the done's. One of the fastest-growing groups in religious America is the none's. These are the people who say they have no religious affiliation. The other group is the done's. These people have left the church, disappointed, and have no plans of returning. God has called us to be salt and light (Matthew 5:13-16). We are called to attract people to our Lord, not repel them.

God wants His people to understand that heaven and the kingdom on earth will always conflict.

Nevertheless, we are to model truth, justice, and righteousness. When Christians live their lives like Christians, we are the most powerful force on the face of the earth. Our responsibility is to keep the main thing being the main thing: Christ, and Christ crucified. That's the political role of the church. **See Footnote 8D, Pages 157-160.**

The method of the Church's impact upon society at large should be twofold. First, the Church must live according to Christian principles and point out where the existing social order conflicts with them. As Dr. Martin Luther King Jr. stated,

"A religion true to its nature must also be concerned about man's social conditions . . . Any religion that professes to be concerned with the souls of men and is not concerned with the slums that damn them, the economic conditions that strangle them, and the social conditions that cripple them is a dry-as-dust religion."

Secondly, the church must pass those principles on to Christian citizens. The task involves reshaping the landscape to one that is closer in conformity to Biblical principles. Accomplishing this will include greater involvement in the political arena. Unedited research data on *racial inequality in the United States* has been documented in **Footnote 8E, Pages 161-170.**

Footnotes – 8A-8E

Footnote 8A – Opportunities to impact social injustice

If our eyes are open, there are unlimited opportunities where we can make an impact on social injustice. It could be our neighbor's children who could benefit from a school breakfast program, a family in your community that encounters unfair treatment from other neighbors, someone in your church family that's being overlooked because of an economic disparity, and/or a cafeteria that fails to consider the dietary norms of a particular culture that frequents it. Your list may not resemble mine, but all of us could easily put one together. Even if there are no disparities in your environment, there are several other social needs around the world that could benefit from our contributions.

In Luke 10:36-38, Jesus asked a salient question at the end of the Samaritan parable,

Which of these three do you think proved to be a neighbor to the man who fell into the hands of the robbers? The one who showed mercy to him, he said. Then Jesus told him, Go and do the same.

He's saying the same to us. Which one of the three reactions does yours most resemble?

Footnote 8B – Consequences of Isolation (*unedited internet discourse*)

The isolation caused by COVID-19 precautions enticed many to engage in the detrimental influences of social media information. Growing numbers of people accepted social media information without any fact-checking. Too often, people either believe what they find through social media or they agree with what they find that aligns with what they previously believed. Either way, the pursuit of truth is ignored.

Footnote 8C – So different, and yet so much alike

In I Samuel 16:7, God says,

But the Lord said unto Samuel, Look not on his countenance, or on the height of his stature; because I have refused him: for the Lord sees not as man does; for man looks on the outward appearance, but the Lord looks at the heart.

What a stark contrast of vision. Too often, our disparities (racial, economic, cultural, gender, ETC.) derive from what we see or perceive from an outer perspective. Our eyes may physically show us the differences in each other. If we take the time to get to know the real person we find that we are more alike in our life pursuits than we are different. If we continue to gravitate to like circumstances, we will not grow in our social development. Moreover, our world will pale in terms of what God has purposed for our lives.

Footnote 8D - Why Christians should be involved in politics.

The following responses were captured from a Grace + Truth project dealing with Christians and political views. I think it reveals many of the challenges we see in our society today.

I don't disagree that Christians should not isolate themselves from "politics." We are ultimately meant to be the salt of the earth and hence meant to bring godly influence to our world. However, there is a caveat. Many Christian leaders who do get involved in politics, such as the US politics, are evangelicals. Some of them have an agenda that could be godly, personal, or a little of both. The latter two agendas are what the problem with Christians getting involved with politics is.

The US had a president who claims to be a Christian yet was blatantly abusive and harsh towards his opponents and the media. This behavior is unacceptable from someone who is supposed to hear the fruit of the Spirit. He had even been accused of sexually assaulting a woman and found to be liable for damages by the grand jury. He had even been videotaped to say sexually crude things about women (about grabbing women's private parts and being proud of it). There are many other things that reflect that consistent behavior.

However, some Christian leaders continue to choose to align with that person and say great things about him. There are times when the "means" do justify the end. But in God's kingdom, whatever the end goal might be, there are those times where we simply cannot jeopardize the sanctity of the church by resorting to "means" that abide with the falsehood just to make sure our "godly" goals are met, sometimes people convince themselves that "it's okay, we can bend the rules a little because we have a critical goal that helps move God's kingdom forward." I believe that is ultimately betraying our Christian faith. Deep down, the root of these kinds of actions is that power corrupts, and the attraction of worldly power will corrupt even the most "holy" and devout Christian leader. Before voting for any candidate, read Proverbs 6 and use it as a measuring stick. What does the Holy Spirit and scripture ask us to do?

He hath shewed thee, O man, what is good; and what doth the Lord require of thee, but to do justly, and to love mercy, and to walk humbly with thy God?

Micah 6:8

This means being concerned for the structures of society which fail to do these things. Why does Israel get instructed on how to order their society? Why did the early church challenge the systems of Empire and coercion? How can we simply stand back and not be engaged in the way our towns, cities, and nations are run? American politics might be a nightmare, and I am not saying we all have to be deeply involved in party politics, but we have to be engaged citizens speaking truth to those in power, seeking to turn our nations from the way of Babylon and be more like the kingdom of God.

I happen to agree with you in general. Many Christians fail to *rightly divide Scripture*, leaning to their own understanding without ceaseless prayer. This becomes an issue when one's inward and imbalanced ego dominates the spiritual person to the point they become self-centered & unloving. Being engaged spiritually betokens holiness and separation from the world system where mere barter is the highest expression of care & concern, rather than *agape*. This is the reason political involvement by believers is so insidious, because leaning to one's own understanding is ever the genesis of unrighteousness. Believers should be engaged in public affairs, but only to the extent the Spirit leads according to the instant guiding of the Spirit and to the Lord's place & time, not our own.

Flying off the handle and doing things the way of Babylon is merely where the ends justify the means, and the Lord God does not operate that way... that's a human failing. The Lord's timing and provision, as with anything else in Christ, are essential to righteousness, not mere right and wrong. Moderation is crucial in this instance, as both religion and politics are emotionally combustible. Combining the two often results in self-serving unrighteousness at the expense of one's witness and the Gospel. If things aren't decent and in order, then they will likely be self-corrupt and disordered. This affects both religion and politics, and especially the two combined. To love your neighbors doesn't mean you have to agree with them. King David wasn't perfect, but he had a heart for God.

Christians should be involved in politics because to do so portrays the Christian life in them. They will give fair justice and good governance to its citizens, which includes the distribution of national resources, provision of social amenities, protection of people's lives and properties, and the creation of a good environment for citizens to live, just as Joseph did in the book of Genesis 44.

Footnote 8E – Racial Disparity

In the United States, racial inequality refers to the social inequality and advantages and disparities that affect different races. The wealth gap between Caucasian and African American families substantially increased from $85,000 in 1984 to $236,500 in 2009.

History

Africans would be captured and brought into the United States as enslaved people, depriving them of all property, and in some cases, family. In order to prevent rebellion or escape, the slave codes in some states banned educating slaves, especially teaching a slave to read or write. Redistribution of land from white owners to the people formerly forced to work it was attempted under the forty acres and a mule policy of Union General William Tecumseh Sherman. This was reversed by President Andrew Johnson. Under slavery, African Americans were treated as property. After the American Civil War, Black sharecroppers became trapped in debt. African Americans were rarely able to homestead. The Freedman's Savings Bank failed, losing many Black assets.

African American farmers did not own land or supplies and had to depend on the White Americans who rented the land and supplies to them. At the same time, southern Blacks were trapped in debt and denied banking services while White citizens were given low-interest loans to set up farms in the Midwest and Western United States. White homesteaders were able to go west and obtain unclaimed land through government grants, while the land grants and rights of African Americans were rarely enforced.

After the Civil War, the Freedman's Bank helped to foster wealth accumulation for African Americans. However, it failed in 1874, partially because of suspicious high-risk loans to White banks and the panic of 1873. This lowered the support African Americans had to open businesses and acquire wealth.

In addition, after the bank failed, taking the assets of many African Americans with it, many African Americans did not trust banks. There was also the threat of lynching to any African American who achieved success.

The Federal Housing Administration and Veteran's Administration shut out African Americans by giving loans to suburbs instead of central cities. Housing segregation caused unequal living standards and poverty. Exclusions from Social Security disproportionately affect African Americans. Racial segregation and racial profiling led to differences in economic disparities.

Economics

Wealth can be defined as "the total value of things families own minus their debts." In contrast, income can be defined as, "earnings from work, interest and dividends, pensions, and transfer payments." Wealth is an important factor in determining the quality of both individual and family life because it can be used as a tool to secure a desired quality of life or class status. It enables individuals who possess it to pass their class status to their children. Family inheritance, which is passed down from generation to generation, helps with wealth accumulation. Wealth can also serve as a safety net against fluctuations in income and poverty.

There is a large gap between the wealth of minority households and white households within the United States. The Pew Research Center's analysis of 2009 government data says the median wealth of white households is 20 times that of Black households and 18 times that of Hispanic households.

According to the Federal Reserve of Cleveland, the wealth gap between white and Black Americans has remained roughly the same since 1962, when the average white family had seven times the wealth of the average Black family. Segregation reduced upward economic mobility.

Health care

Black Americans face consistently worse health outcomes than White, Asian, and Hispanic Americans. Black women are 2½ times more likely to die of maternal causes than White women and this rate increases to 3 times when compared to Hispanic Americans. The infant mortality rate for Black Americans is 11 per 1,000 births which is higher than the US average of 5.7.

Housing segregation

Housing segregation in the United States is the practice of denying African American or other minority group's equal access to housing through the process of misinformation, denial of realty and financing services, and racial steering. The effects of housing segregation include relocation difficulties, unequal living standards, and overty. However, there have been initiatives to combat housing segregation, such as the Section 8 housing program. Racial residential segregation is a fundamental cause of racial disparities in health. Racial segregation can result in decreased opportunities for minority groups in income, education, and other critical life sustaining areas.

Residential segregation and poverty concentration are most markedly seen in the comparison between urban and suburban populations. Suburbs consist of White majority populations, and inner-cities consist of minority majority populations. According to Barnhouse-Walters (2001), the concentration of poor minority populations in inner-cities and the concentration of affluent white populations in the suburbs "is the main mechanism by which racial inequality in educational resources is reproduced."

Education

In the United States, funding for public education relies greatly on local property taxes. Local property tax revenues may vary between different neighborhoods and school districts. This variance of property tax revenues amongst neighborhoods and school districts leads to inequality in education. The average nonwhite school district receives $2,226 less than a white school district per student enrolled.

Crime rates and incarceration

In 2008, the prison population under federal and state correctional jurisdiction was over 1,610,446 prisoners. Of these prisoners, 20% were Hispanic (compared to 16.3% of the U.S. population that is Hispanic), 34% were White (compared to 63.7% of the U.S. population that is White), and 38% were Black (compared to 12.6% of the U.S. population that is Black). Additionally, Black males were imprisoned at a rate 6.5 times higher than that of their White male counterparts.

Consequences of a criminal record

The injustices of a criminal justice system disproportionately impact Black people and continuing these racial disparities has a high cost for individuals, families, and communities. On an individual level, a criminal conviction may equate to loss of access to employment, housing, and public service opportunities. Over 40 percent who are released will return to prison within the next few years. Those with criminal records who do not return to prison face significant struggles to find quality employment and income compared to those who do not have criminal records.

Several sociological studies have found that poor offenders receive longer sentences for violent crimes and crimes involving drug use, unemployed offenders are more likely to be incarcerated than their employed counterparts, and similar crimes and criminal records have shown that minorities were imprisoned more often than whites.

Racial profiling

Racial profiling is defined as "any police-initiated action that relies on the race, ethnicity, or national origin, rather than the behavior of an individual or information that leads the police to a particular individual who has been identified as being, or having been, engaged in criminal activity." A report by the *National Registry of Exonerations* found that *African Americans* were seven times more likely to be falsely convicted compared to White Americans.

Police brutality

Police brutality in the United States is defined as "the unwarranted or excessive and often illegal use of force against civilians by U.S. police officers. It can come in the form of murder, assault, mayhem, or torture, as well as less physical means of violence, including general harassment, verbal abuse, and intimidation. During peaceful protests for civil rights, some police would use tactics such as police dogs or fire hoses to control protesters. In 1991, video footage was released of cab driver Rodney King being hit over 50 times by multiple police with their batons. The police were later acquitted for their actions which resulted in the 1992 Los Angeles riots. Allegations of police brutality continue to plague American police.

Black Americans are 2–3 times more likely to be killed in a police shooting than White Americans and are more likely to be unarmed during those fatal instances. The study found that armed Black men were shot more frequently than armed White men and were also shot more quickly. The police would also sometimes mistakenly shoot the unarmed Black targets, while neglecting to shoot the armed White targets.

Color-blind racism

United States has now switched to a new form of racism known as color-blind racism. Color-blind racism refers to contemporary racial inequality as the outcome of nonracial dynamics. Those practices are not racially overt in nature such as racism under slavery, segregation, and Jim Crow laws. Instead, color-blind racism flourishes on the idea that race is no longer an issue in the country and that there are non-racial explanations for the state of inequality. Eduardo Bonilla-Silva writes that there are four frames of color-blind racism that support that view:

1. Abstract liberalism uses ideas associated with political liberalism. This frame is based in liberal ideas such as equal opportunity, individualism, and choice. It uses these ideas as a basis to explain inequality.

2. Naturalization explains racial inequality as a cause of natural occurrences. It claims that segregation is not the result of racial dynamics. Instead, it is the result of the naturally-occurring phenomena of individuals choosing likeness as their preference.

3. Cultural racism explains racial inequality through culture. Under this frame, racial inequalities are described as the result of stereotypical behavior of minorities. Stereotypical behavior includes qualities such as laziness and teenage pregnancy.

4. Minimization of racism attempts to minimize the factor of race as a major influence in affecting the life chances of minorities. It writes off instances and situations that could be perceived as discrimination to be hypersensitive to the topic of race.

Credit scores

Credit score systems are well known to contain racial

bias and have been shown to increase racial disparities. Studies show that African American and American Latino populations have substantially lower scores than the White American population on average.

Various studies showing racial disparities in credit scoring:

- 1996 study found African-Americans were three times as likely to have FICO scores below 620 as Whites and that Hispanics were twice as likely.

- 1997 study found Black, Indigenous, and people of color (BIPOC) neighborhood consumers had lower credit scores.

- 2004 study found high Black, Indigenous, and other people of color (BIPOC) zip codes to have significantly worse scores than non-Black, Indigenous, and people of color (BIPOC) zip codes.

- 2004 study found that African American and Hispanic consumers constituted over 60% of the consumers having the worst credit scores.

- 2012 study examined the credit scores for about 200,000 consumers finding the median FICO score in majority minority zip codes was in the 34th percentile, while it was in the 52nd percentile for low minority zip codes.

As a result, the outcomes for Black Americans because of this bias are higher interest rates on home loans and auto loans, longer loan terms, increased debt collection default lawsuits, and an increase in the use of predatory lenders.

Chapter 9
Summary

━━━➤━━━━━━━━━━━━━━━━━━━◄━━━

For in the same way that one body has so many different parts, each with different functions; we, too being many are different parts that form one body in the Anointed One. Each one of us is joined with one another, and we become together what we could not be alone.

Romans 12:4-5

In the introduction section of this book, I shared that I have over forty years of experience in ministry. **See Footnote 9A, Page 196.** During those 40-plus years, several men and women of God poured into my life and ministry. I listed those individuals in the acknowledgment section. I want to share a nugget with you about each of those mighty men and women of courage. For me, they were the living stones that collectively aided in my development. Most importantly, they were organized and orchestrated by God. Through the power of the Holy Spirit, they produced Kairos moments in my ministry. A Kairos moment is a God orchestrated experience when conditions are optimal and the opportunity is favorable.

In 1983, I confessed God's calling on my life. I was raised in the church as an infant, so the church life was not new to me. I attended Sunday school, Baptist Training Unit (BTU), laymen's ministry, Young adult and adult usher board, choir, and other support areas. As important as each of those ministries is, they did not have the impact on my life that the preaching ministry did. I did not want to be a shyster in ministry; in fact, I didn't want to be in ministry. After unsuccessfully trying to ignore and deny the calling, I surrendered.

I had an advantage that many beginning ministers don't have. My Pastor, the late Dr. Samuel M. Edwards, was a learned man who was very kind and compassionate. His focus was always on the family. I always remembered that from my youth. When Pastor Alvin Hawkins succeeded him, he didn't possess the academic degrees, but he overflowed with life experience, wisdom, and common sense. He shared his time and experience with the associate ministers. I spent as much time as I could with him. There were also several associates whose ministry experience ranged from 3 – 40 years.

I learned from Eugene Jones (full of wisdom and discipline), Billie D. Allen (one of my greatest teachers), Lee Turner (a true and transparent friend), James Pittman (one of the most dependable, reliable, and faithful ministers there), Gary Williamson (my biological brother who taught me and kept me humble), and William Bell Jr. (my brother-in-law who embodied Proverbs 27:17). Pastor Bell also accompanied me on our first trip to the Holy Land in 2019. If a minister failed to be relevant coming out of LMBC, it was certainly not because the training wasn't available to them.

The associate ministers were exposed to great pastors with decades of experience. They would always share wisdom with us to help us grow. Dr. Bailey, Dr. Goodwin, and Dr. Hockenhull conducted workshops for ministry growth and development. When we ministers could get them alone, we would take advantage of those times to ask what we thought were challenging questions. With seemingly no effort, they would share simplistic and understandable answers that left us in awe. Bailey shared structure, Goodwin emphasized kindness, and Hockenhull was heavily focused on stewardship.

Dean, Dr. S. J. Williams was my first academic instructor in ministry. My brother said, *"If you're going to be solid in your preaching and teaching, you should enroll at Detroit Bible College with the rest of us."* That was the best decision I made in ministry. Dean Williams helped me establish substance in ministry. He planted so many salient seeds that I will never forget. He shared so many simple truths with the ministers. I don't know how much of an impact he had on them, but his teaching was revolutionary for me. He was a very simplistic man of God but possessed wisdom untold. **See Footnote 9B, Pages 196-197.**

During my first year in ministry, I met Charles Thompson in my workplace. Charles taught a Bible study during the break. I thought this would be an opportunity to learn more about the Bible. Charles and I became the best of friends. Under his tutelage and spending time together, he allowed me to alternate teaching the Bible class when he wasn't available. I learned so much from the questions asked and discovered how unbelievably knowledgeable he was to be as young as he was.

I later met Will Cain and Wilbert Whatley. These two pastors transferred to our facility when my ministry was stale. A lot had happened in my life, and I wasn't growing. I was kind of treading water. These were the right two brothers at the right time; Kairos time. It wasn't long before they reinvigorated my thirst for learning and service. I became Wilbert's assistant pastor and Will Cain ordained me.

Another foundational stone of encouragement has been how God has blessed me with pastors throughout my family. I have an uncle (Jessie), cousins (Bruce, Darryl, and Clintina), another brother (Daniel), a sister (Gail), and brother-in-law (Earl) who have provided support and encouragement, and have challenged me to study deeper. There was a time in ministry when I was taught that God didn't call women into ministry. Some of the most effective ministry work I've witnessed has been in the ministry work of women. If we are going to be effective in honoring Jesus's commission in Matthew 28:18-20, we will have to go beyond the four walls of our church buildings and the personal thoughts we hold if they don't align themselves with the Word of God.

In 2002, I met Pastor Gabrielle Lewis. He pastored Second New Hope Church in Michigan. I was interviewing him for a thesis project. One question that I remember asking him was, "How do you effectively manage all of the responsibilities that come with such a diverse group of people, and at such a dynamic time in our society?" I did not expect the response I was given. He said that in times past, pastors could reasonably address the concerns of the church body. He said today, we live in a more sophisticated world. He realized that he didn't have all of the answers, so he utilized the professional talents of those God had sent to him. It's a shared effort. That's what you don't see a lot of today, pastors willing to share their spotlight.

A few years later, I united with Second New Hope under the pastoral leadership of Eric Burr. Pastor Burr is one of the most humble pastors I know. Through this ministry, I met his brother James E Burr (Biblically solid), nephew James A Burr (more gifted than he realizes), Michael Harris (a true friend for life), Tracey Pollard, David Simmons, William Harper, and John Williams who are a true depiction of what brotherhood looks like in ministry. These seven years were the best years of my ministry. I later met Pastor Vincent Wolf, who is a builder of men and a commercial builder of church buildings. We attended conferences all over the country. We assisted in helping hurricane victims from New Orleans, Orlando, Baton Rough, and local community endeavors.

In 2006, Pastor Eric Burr organized a Man Up, Mountain Top Men's conference in Midland, Michigan. He incorporated a group of speakers that rocked our world. The list included Dr. E.L. Branch (a preaching machine), Pastor Hamon Cross Jr. (an in-your-face challenger), Pastor Gabrielle Lewis (real life, raw challenge), Pastor Everett Jennings (maintaining leadership stamina), Pastor Jake Gaines (thought provoking), Pastor James Minnick (a down to earth organizer), Pastor Kelvin Burton (medical doctor - men's health), Pastor Reginald Smith (finance guru), and Ellis Liddell (financial advisor). Every aspect of Christian living was represented by these great men of God. This conference was held annually for years. These men transformed every aspect of our lives.

In 2010, my wife and I relocated to Fort Wayne, Indiana. After about a year, we united with the Greater Progressive Church. Pastor Anthony R. Pettus was the pastor. Through that ministry, I developed a deeper understanding of God's Word. Pastor Pettus gave me a Bible Study program that took my study to another level. On the job, I met Pastor Bill Robinson, who brought me into the chaplaincy where I later served as

Chaplain Chair for the UAW. While serving in the UAW Chaplaincy, I met the Chaplaincy leaders, Elders Jerry Carson, and Herb Taylor. Jerry and Herb exposed me to a broader aspect of ministry. It was during these years that I learned how broad the responsibilities of chaplains are. I was allowed to teach a leadership class at one of our chaplain's conferences. I am grateful for that experience. While in Indiana, I met Pastor Anthony Payton (pastor, entrepreneur, and ministry developer), and Bishop Crystal Thomas, our keynote speaker at one of our chaplaincy luncheons. Bishop Thomas made a statement that I have applied to my life ever since – *"Whatever you touch in life, leave it better than you found it."* Similar to a quote from Mother Teresa: "Be kind and merciful. Let no one ever come to you without coming away better and happier."

In 2017, I retired and relocated to eastern Tennessee. As we searched for a church family, we united with Mt Canaan in Chattanooga, Tennessee. We planned to find a home in middle Tennessee, but God had another Kairos moment for us. Unbeknown to us, we ended up at Mt. Canaan where the Pastor, Ternae Jordan Sr., was the former pastor of the church we left in Fort Wayne, Indiana. Being a strange man in a strange land, I needed a friend in ministry, and that's just what God had orchestrated. In making my decision to retire, I made two requests to God. Send me where I can give you full-time service utilizing the skills and gifts you've given me, and take care of my finances. He has more than honored that request.

Pastor Jordan has been more than a friend, and he has connected me with so many resourceful men and women of God. I share ministerial responsibilities with 20 other ministers within the church. I assisted one of them (Min. Morris Beaty) in teaching a Bible study for seniors. He later recommended that I be put in the rotation, so now I teach once a month. Pastor Jordan introduced me to Pastor Micah Fries, Pastor Dennis Culbreath, Pastor Gus Hernandez, and Dr. Willie McLaurin. These men are, or were a part of the Tennessee Baptist Association. Micah Fries is one of the most personable pastors I've met. Dennis and Gus have provided countless resources necessary to complete many ministry initiatives. Willie organized a trip to the Holy Land, enabling me to fulfill a life-long dream. I was honored to be a part of that tour group.

The last four Men are major contributors to my biblical studies. I have personally met three of the four men. Their written and spoken words have provided comfort, growth, and development, just when I needed them most. When we were searching for a home in Tennessee, Mt. Zion is where we would attend Sunday services before returning to Indiana. I met both Bishop Walker and Bishop Paul Morton at Mt Zion. I replayed their CDs when I needed to hear a timely word. Dr. John MacArthur is one of my favorite writers. He's one of the few authors whose material I purchase simply because of his authorship. I have never been disappointed. I met Dr. Tony Evans a couple of times. I have been blessed by the Tony Evans Bible version. His Bible has added much clarity in areas where I needed greater understanding.

I thought it was important to share my experience with these great men and women of God. I wanted to reinforce the importance of recognizing the people that God has placed in our lives. They are all conducive to our transformation. I am so grateful for every ounce of wisdom, time, and words of encouragement each of these individuals provided me. Time is our greatest commodity, and the time all of you have given me have not been taken for granted.

In summary, I want to point out again that successful churches operate within a system that embodies the purpose given to that assembly. Its goals, mission, and direction are aimed toward the objectives. The journey requires us to focus on the organizing aspects of the church. We were reminded that the church belongs to God. The church was purchased with the precious blood of Jesus that was shed for it. We pointed out that *the church is not the buildings we worship in, it is the called-out assembly of born-again believers.* This called-out group is comprised of all kinds of people from all walks of life.

Therefore, all preparation, arrangements, structure, coordination, and delegation must include and involve the doctrines, beliefs, principles, and precepts of God's Word.

While God often gives the unction to one person to start a church, He also provides countless others to assist in carrying out the assignment. The harvest is truly plentiful and the laborers needed are sometimes difficult to find, but God always provides where He guides. Organizers can benefit from the wise counsel of other organizers who have failed and succeeded in prior endeavors. Church organizers must possess good leadership skills. There is a variety of leadership styles. It is vitally important for a leader to know the style and skills he possesses and understands how he can best utilize those skills to aid in the organizing effort. It also helps with determining what skills may be necessary to recruit. Moreover, he must be sure of his calling. When God calls us to an assignment, He will see it through. There will be obstacles and challenges, but is there anything too difficult for God?

In Matthew 16:18, Jesus said unto Peter, *Upon This Rock*, I will build My Church. We clarified that the *Rock* upon which He was referring to is Himself, not Peter. We learned that the word He used was *Petra* which is defined as a collection of rocks. Thus, Jesus's church would include His unified followers who would confess Him as the Christ, the Son of the living God, just as Peter did. Christ is both the Founder of the church and the Foundation; it is He that draws souls, and He draws them to Himself.

The Hebrew meaning of the word rock is – firmness, stability, and faithfulness. Those words describe our Savior, not Peter. Jesus further clarifies that the church that He builds upon a rock is His church. In Acts 20:28, Luke says regarding the church –

Here are my instructions: diligently guard yourselves, and diligently guard the whole flock over which the Holy Spirit has given you oversight. Shepherd the church of God, this precious church which He made His own through the blood of His own Son.

We all sometimes claim ownership of our churches. We refer to them as my church or our church. In the spirit of what we mean, that's a healthy statement. We are affectionately attaching ourselves to a particular assembly of believers. However, in its truest sense, the church belongs to God. He has full ownership, and what a blessing that is because He goes further and declares, *The Gates of Hell Shall Not Prevail Against It.* If you or I made that declaration based on our ownership of the church, it wouldn't carry much weight. However, when Jesus declares it that settles it. He is more than capable of sustaining not only the church but every part of His creation. As John 1:3, and Psalm 55:22 states,

All things were made by him; and without him was not anything made that was made.

Cast thy burden upon the Lord, and he shall sustain thee: he shall never suffer the righteous

to be moved.

When Jesus promised that the gates of hell would not prevail or overtake the church, He was not implying that Satan would stop his efforts to alter and destroy it. The church has a God-given and God-established purpose, and that purpose doesn't require Satan's assistance. That, however, hasn't discouraged or distracted him from trying. Satan uses every trick and gimmick available to negatively influence God's people. As I have explained several times throughout this book, **God's called-out people are the church, not the building in which they worship Him.** Jesus intended that every believer would be equipped with the spiritual tools needed to fulfill their God-given purpose. **See Footnote 9C, Pages 197-198.**

I have expressed the importance of the church from a holistic perspective. I believe "all" phases of a parishioner's life should be addressed within the church. The church body should be the safest and most trusting resource available to believers. If the church cannot be trusted to equip the saints with spiritual and civil life skills, where else should they seek to find these qualities? Jesus's intent for the church is to show support for one another through honoring, encouraging, loving, and showing compassion for each other. The purpose of the church is to be the believer's spiritual family. It is through the church that God takes people with different personalities and gifts, unifies them as a single body, and equips them to care for each other to reach the world.

The church is the medium God uses today to display to the world what it looks like to live under a righteous government, ruled by a sovereign King. It is incumbent upon the church to reflect a righteous government and not an evil dictatorship. Too many churches are utilizing their power and influence to effect change in matters that God did not call us to do. Our purpose is to first establish and develop an intimate relationship with God. We then go out and impact our inner circles (our families and our church families, friends, neighbors, and close associates.) Our last endeavor is where we go out to the highways and byways, to the outer regions of the world when this is the assignment that God gives. This is our "Up, In, and Out." **See footnote 9D, Pages 198-200.**

In Chapter 4, I revealed that obstacles and challenges will continuously confront the church. Most, if not all of them, can be seen in one of these ten categories:

1. Mobilizing for evangelism

2. Concern for evangelism

3. Retaining young adults

4. Leadership burnout

5. Member mobilization

6. Effects of social media

7. Member bible knowledge

8. Present-day sexual ethics

9. Member indifference

10. Community outreach

The best antidotes I can offer is to keep God's agenda your priority and to focus on the assignment He has called upon your assembly. So often, church groups become distracted by what's working in other assemblies. I call that, *"being enticed by shiny objects."* William Shakespeare said it this way, *"All that glitters is not gold"*, not everything that looks precious or true turns out to be so. When churches chase the assignments of other churches, they struggle and often fail. When we stay true to what God has assigned, He will see it through (Phil. 1:6).

Perhaps our greatest challenge within the church is ourselves. God has provided direction and assurance to defeat all the issues associated with the ten challenges above. When we, however, become insensitive, unaffected, disconnected, and apathetic about challenges to the church, we become our internal challenge. In Revelation, John categorizes these kinds of believers as "lukewarm." The challenge for lukewarm people is that it produces indifference. They possess just enough Bible knowledge to negate resistance but not enough real faith to become completely engaged. It is much more difficult to convert a lukewarm person (*indifferent*) than a cold person. In Revelation 3:16, John says that God will vomit a lukewarm person out of His mouth. Indifferent believers are destructive to the church.

The separation and isolation that COVID-19 created for church gatherings have affected people returning to the church building. For decades, before COVID-19, parishioners were cautioned against replacing in-person church attendance with cyber attendance. Many leaders reminded their church of Hebrews 10:25 which speaks to the importance of believer's fellowshipping with each other. Nevertheless, many church members have not returned to the church building. Leaders may fare better with efforts to create small-group studies to reconnect with these members and use some of those opportunities to jointly put a plan together for their return.

Another area where churches are challenged is Finances and Budgeting. It should be clearly understood that church money and other church resources belong to the church and not to any individual, including pastors! The financial contributions of members of a church are meant to meet the needs and obligations of the church. Another important factor regarding financial accountability in the church is the understanding that church funds are not just meant for the upkeep of pastors alone. Church funds are there to address all church needs and those of the House of God. Those financial contributions should not only include taking care of the ministers of the gospel but also provide for the maintenance of the poor and needy, widows, the fatherless, and others who need assistance.

Tithing is a concept that has to be taught. If your church's method of teaching tithing is reading the instructions given by Malachi and Luke, the giving might be more from compulsion than from the heart. Whatever method the church decides to use for funding the church, consistency in following it is a must. The money that flows through the church is used to support its operations and to cover all other financial responsibilities, including staff salaries, ministry activities, maintaining the infrastructure of the church, community engagement activities, and the salaries of church leaders.

How does the church adequately pay the pastor? The pastor's salary is always a challenging topic in the church world. There is no single answer to this question. Every church is different, and the role of each pastor is equally unique. Both the role of the pastor and the resources for payment vary from church to church. The circumstances will determine what appropriate pay is for the pastor. The more effort put into the planning and forecasting phase, the clearer the picture will be regarding what qualities the church needs to finish well. It is also better to be as transparent as possible when considering the future direction of the church. Churches should reevaluate all aspects of church expenses every year. This practice aids in avoiding common mistakes, such as increasing compensation solely because of tenure or allowing emotions to override facts.

The church family's ability to fund programs should be the determining factor in supporting its endeavors. God's church is expected to be a group of called-out people in relationships who live life together. Relationships are vital because the expectations of God's purposes are realized and demonstrated within those relationships. Church leaders also have a responsibility for the development of the church family. God has given them the responsibility to serve, equip, and develop others within the church family. They are called to nourish the holistic and spiritual needs of their members. Their agenda should include providing them with viable resources to navigate the struggles encountered in their generation. **See Footnote 9E, Page 200.**

God has promised to provide everything necessary to sustain His church. Sometimes that will include recruitment of resources outside of the church family. This might involve developing relationships with the community that shares a common interest with the church. Recruitment also provides an opportunity to witness to those in our communities who may not be a part of God's Christian family. All of us were outside of the family of God at some point. Skills, talents, and resources are abundant outside of the church, and through effective witnessing, those resources can be utilized while offering them salvation. Many of those people may not be opposed to the Christian life; it may be that they just haven't been introduced to it. Shared civil values can lead to shared Christian values. **See Footnote 9F, Page 200-201.**

Education and training, whether secular or spiritual, remain a critical component of church growth and development. Jesus is our greatest example of Christian ministry, but He also had a secular profession. The Bible tells us that He was a carpenter (Mark Ch. 6). Many of His disciples were fishermen.

Now as Jesus walked by the Sea of Galilee, he saw Simon and Andrew his brother casting a net into the sea: for they were fishers. And Jesus said unto them, Come ye after me, and I will make you to become fishers of men.

Mark 1:16-17

Paul was a tentmaker by trade.

Paul moved in with them, and they worked together at their common trade of tent-making.

Acts 18:3

In addition to our church family responsibilities, we have a responsibility to our families as well. Jesus, the disciples, and Paul were effective in ministry, but they also had a secular profession. They were educated and trained. We must do the same. We must not only prepare ourselves for meaningful work but also identify and prepare others. Some will show signs of technical ability where others may be more academically inclined. Our responsibility is to recognize those skills and give them the best chance at fulfilling them. These skills can be used to edify the church.

Education and training are additionally important because they provide the opportunity to train the younger generation how to think, process, and make practical decisions throughout life. Our job is not to teach them *"what"* to think; we teach them *"how"* to think. I believe tithing is a great start for financially supporting the church. I recommend a 10, 10, 80 money management practice. Ten percent to the kingdom, ten percent to personal savings, and eighty percent to support your lifestyle. Ten percent personal savings is a good baseline, but successful investing must include financial education and training. We should know why we tithe and what and with whom we are investing our savings. God does more for the

Church with our 10% of giving than we do for ourselves with the 90% that remains. Give what God requires first, live your life based on 80%, and trust

God to multiply the 10% you invest. Eventually, you will give more than 10% to kingdom work.

Jesus reminds us in Matthew 6:31-33 –

So do not consume yourselves with questions: What will we eat? What will we drink? What will we wear? 32 Outsiders make themselves frantic over such questions; they don't realize that your heavenly Father knows exactly what you need. 33 Seek first the kingdom of God and His righteousness, and then all these things will be given to you too.

The same principle should be used for all areas of life. Spending, diet, schooling, marriage, family, vehicle purchases, travel, whatever you spend money on, it should first be filtered through an education and training process. That's a holistic perspective and good stewardship. **See footnote 9F, page X.**

The ruler replied, "Well done! You're a good servant indeed! Since you have been faithful in handling a small amount of money, I'll entrust you with authority over 10 cities in my new kingdom."

Luke 19:17

In Chapter 8, I presented a lengthy discourse on the social and political responsibilities of the church. I won't be as wordy in my summary, but I will make a few salient points. I addressed the topic of social responsibility with Jesus's response to the lawyer in Luke 10:25-37. The lawyer asked the question, "Who Is My Neighbor?" From that discourse, we understood that our neighbor is anyone we show neighborly kindness and compassion. That is the church's social obligation. That is also the problem that plagues our society. I have never seen a time when the first assessment of so many people is to look for something they can oppose. Too many in our society focus on others' perceived weaknesses rather than an obvious strength they possess. If no one else can see the need for a change, the church must. Yes, we are our brother's keeper. Yes, I need you, and you need me because we are all a part of God's family.

None of us should be OK with an injustice of any kind. Conversely, we should all strive for justice when an opportunity presents itself. It is vitally important that we model this behavior for future generations. In so many of my experiences, the younger generation has a better handle on social interaction than we do. When the tragedy of 9-11 occurred, those hoping to be rescued did not care what age, gender, race, or economic background their rescuer was, they were just thankful for their sacrifice. We are experiencing devastating hurricanes as I'm writing. Those affected by them are desperate for assistance. How neighborly would it be to assess the racial or economic status of those in need before we offer help?

Warner Bros. produced a movie in 1996 titled *A Time To Kill*. The Movie takes place in a segregated southern town. Two white men raped a little black girl, and her father shot and killed them both. A guilty verdict was expected. In the closing statement, a white lawyer, who was representing the black father, retold the horrific story, step by step, of what took place with this little black girl. The jury was almost emotionless. Just as he was finishing the story, he said these words – *"Now, imagine that this little girl was white!"*

The jury returned with a not-guilty verdict. A black man murdered two white men and admitted he did it, and the only reason the jury found him not guilty is because they realized that if the girl had been their white daughter, they would have killed the two white men, too. We have to be better than that. The church, if nowhere else, must elevate its social empathy for all mankind, regardless of race, gender, etc. Murder is wrong no matter who commits it. Having two sets of determining factors based on who commits the murder is equally unjust.

The political responsibility of the church was presented in the form of a question – *Should the Church be involved in Politics?* The separation of church and state is a political and legal concept that defines the relationship between the government and religious organizations. The world Jesus commissions us to reach *(Matthew 28:18-20)* with the good news is often seen running away from us, not because they reject the claims of Jesus or the church but because they can't tolerate the politics and hypocrisy of those who profess to be followers of Christ.

This doesn't mean that Christians should not have a political view or remain silent and avoid all political discussions. It means that we should compassionately and discernably choose when to have those conversations. Avoiding all political discourse and engagement is quietly supporting the status quo.

The most significant problem today with Christians and politics is not political apathy; it is the over-consumption and obsession with political matters. Our identity in Christ affects how we see everything and everyone. If the gospel we preach is not powerful enough to break down the dividing walls of hostility between Republican Christians and Democratic Christians, is it really the gospel?

The year 2024 is an election year. Christians and non-Christians vote. I agree with those who speak to the importance of each vote. The right to vote was bought with the precious blood of so many past patriots and human rights activists. To carelessly or callously ignore and take that right for granted is unacceptable to me. I disagree with that behavior, but I do understand.

Not too long ago, candidates ran on their promises and accomplishments. If you favored their platform, you gave them your vote. Things have drastically changed in recent campaigns. The strategy now seems to be: determine what your opponent's platform is, and do all you can to destroy it and them. The most effective method in controlling people is to seek out their God (what they believe most and rely on) and then destroy that image while replacing it with yourself or your image of choice. Truth is not critically important in this endeavor. For the right price, you can get almost anyone to support your views. Right or wrong, keep repeating it until it's accepted as truth, or fatigue wears through their resistance. **See Footnote 9G, Pages 201-202.**

I do have a concern with politics and the church. Some political decisions have a significant impact on the church. The church has a responsibility to provide unbiased political education for its members. I believe the church can, and should go so far as to encourage voting. Every church I have been engaged with included members who either held a political office or worked in the political arena. These people can be used to educate your church family. No one should be voting uninformed. That is a disgrace. My other concern is church leaders who tell their people for whom to vote. I don't support the concept of letting your conscience be your guide. There are so many conscienceless, cold-hearted, me-only citizens today, and I don't trust their conscience.

I think everyone should be truthfully informed of candidates' past and present accomplishments and what their plans are. Each voter has a right to believe, agree, accept, or reject a candidate based on their perception of the candidate's integrity. The church must remember that when voting for man's government, we are still accountable to God for our decisions. Our vote should not always reflect what's best for us individually. Our vote should promote what's best for God's kingdom order. Ultimately, we must trust in God and His completed work through the death, burial, and resurrection of His Son, Jesus Christ.

When the church adopts a holistic approach to ministry, it fulfills its prophetic role in society. That is what the church did in Acts 2, and in this divisive era in which we live, that is what the church needs to do today. Implementing all of the concepts and ideas within this book will not produce a perfect church. There is no "perfect church." Remember, the church is not the building you worship in, it's the imperfect called-out Assembly of God's people. Within this book, however, are Biblical foundational principles and practices. They will guide you in building the right structure for your calling. They will provide your church family the best opportunity for establishing growth, development, and fruitfulness. In addition, they will guide you in honoring God's calling and purpose for your church family. You don't have to worry about failure. Jesus said,

Upon This Rock, I Will Build My Church; and The Gates of Hell Shall Not Prevail Against It.

Footnotes – 9A-9G

Footnote 9A – Experience in ministry

One of my mentors told me a story about a pastor who was retiring. The church allowed him to pick his successor. He had three associate ministers. One of them had been with him one year, another one three years, and the other, ten years. The minister who had worked under his leadership for ten years thought it was obvious that he would be the successor. When the minister with one year of experience was chosen, the ten ear veteran asked his pastor why he chose the minister with one year of experience when he had ten. He was told, "You don't have ten years of experience, you have one year of experience, ten times. The minister with one year of experience has grown more in one year than you have the entire ten years you've been with me." I have learned over my forty years in ministry that growth is not predicated on how many years of service you pile up, it's the diversity of people you expose yourself to and the growth realized during those years in ministry.

Footnote 9B – Ministry and Family

Dean Williams shared advice on wisdom and survival in ministry. He told us that in ministry, you are going to encounter opposition from all areas of life.

He said if you are a bi-vocational minister, your job is going to beat up on you when you're out in society or even in the church, there will be those who'll beat up on you. For those reasons alone, ministers must strive to make their homes a safe place. If you establish your home as a safe place, even when the job, world, or church beat up on you, your family will enable you to survive it all. I have found that to be true.

Footnote 9C – 12 Topics for Developmental

These 12 topics were shared with me by one of my mentors (*Pastor Ternae Jordan*). These topics (*when studied and applied*), will challenge your thinking and impact your spiritual and civil development from a holistic perspective.

(Continue to the following page)

12 Topics for Development

1. Who Am I? (Our Image and Dominion - Genesis 1:26)

2. My Perception (The Way I Think – Proverbs 23:7)

3. Male Responsibility (What We Must Do - Galatians 6:5)

4. Iron Sharpens Iron – (Men Strengthening Men - Proverbs 27:17)

5. Loving Eve – (Christ-like Love - Ephesians 5:25)

6. Father/Son Relationship – (Connection & Sacrifice - Luke 2:49)

7. Brotherhood/Gangs – (Discipling – Matthew 13:36)

8. Vision – (Knowing Where You're Going - Habakkuk 2:2)

9. Discipline/Character – (Integrity Building – Hebrews 12:11)

10. Pass It On – (Our Legacy – Proverbs 13:22)

11. Priesthood – (Priest, Protector, Provider – I Peter 2:9)

12. Group Mentoring – (Impacting Our World - Luke 9:23-25)

Footnote 9D – Ministry Triangle

The Up, In, and Out model was presented as a disciple-making concept. It was developed by the 3DM Movement ministry. It reflects Jesus's ministry. Jesus began His ministry demonstrating the importance of His relationship with His Father *"the Up."* After receiving and knowing His assignment (not before), He then was prepared for it. *Perhaps He desired to help as many people as possible, but He only did what His Father decreed (John 5:30).* His assignment was to pour God's purposes for man into His inner circle, *His disciples.* That was His *"In."* His next assignment was to go out into the community and demonstrate God's work to those in the community: *"His Out."*

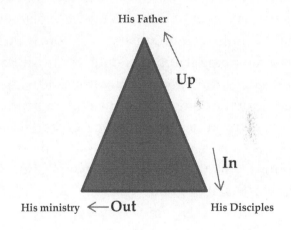

That is the same model for us. We are to develop our relationship with the Father first, discerning our purpose in the process. Then we are to fulfill our purpose in our inner circle: *our families, friends, and those closest to us.* Once we have accomplished that, we are instructed to go throughout the land and baptize, teach, and make disciples of men and women wherever our ministry work takes us (Matthew 28:18-20). That's our Up, In, and Out ministry triangle.

Footnote 9E – Financial Management

Money is a vehicle that drives so many aspects of our lives. Poor money management has impacted living conditions, credit scores, health conditions, and the believer's ability to tithe. In addition, it has destroyed marriages and families. God's purpose for wealth is for us to experience the freedom to do what we choose. When our heart is in the right place, we can do that without compromising our core values and advance the mission and mandate of Christ. Freedom without God's direction is dangerous. Seeking God's purpose provides guardrails as we use our freedom in a way that protects us and also serves His greater purpose. As adults with financial issues, most banking institutions will provide the education and training necessary to stabilize our finances. As parents and guardians, we must find ways (through schools, churches, or at home) to educate our children before they enter the financial decision-making stages of their lives.

Footnote 9F – Recruiting in ministry

I met Pastor Lewis after attending a Sunday service where he pastored. I was working on a thesis project that focused on Transformational Leadership. I noticed his congregation was male-dominant. In the church environment, male-dominant congregations are uncommon. I asked if he would allow me to interview him, and he agreed. I first asked him why there were so many men in his congregation. He shared with me his lifestyle when he was living in the world. Many of the men in his congregation were men with whom he had prior relationships. When they observed the transformation in his life, they kept coming. Sometimes, when people see what God has done in your life, they are willing to see if God will do the same for them. I am a witness that He did. Many of them are still actively a part of that church. Some are professional people, others are dependable and reliable workers in God's vineyard, but they are assets to the kingdom. God provides what we need, but we must reach out to these people.

Footnote 9G – Conquer and Destroy

Some reliable institutions have a proven track record, and their viability is commonly accepted throughout our country. The American Journal of Medicine, pastors, parents, educational institutions, and many others are just a few. These commonly accepted institutions have been replaced by organizations such as Google, Facebook, Twitter, and others. Uninformed people are basing their life decisions on the opinions of social media instead of proven tested factual data. There is only one reliable source that the church should be relying on, and that's the Word of God. Everything else is fallible!

Contributing Sources

Evans, Dr. Tony. *The Tony Evans Bible Commentary*.

Fulgham, Nicole Baker. *Educating All God's Children*.

Horton, David. *The Portable Seminary*.

Hull, Bill. *Conversion & Discipleship – You Can't Have One Without The Other*.

MacArthur, Dr. John. *Twelve Ordinary Men*

Maxwell, John. *Leadership 101*.

McGee, J Vernon. *Thru The Bible – vol. 1-5*

McMickle, Marvin A. *Pulpit & Politics*.

Miller, Mark. *Chess Not Checkers: Elevate Your Leadership Game*.

Munroe, Dr. Miles. *Understanding the Purpose and Power of Men*.

Parrot, Leslie. *Future Church: How Congregations Choose Their Character & Destiny*.

Satrape, Ron. *Retooling the Church: Finding Your Place In Ministry*.

Schnase, Robert. *Five Practices of Fruitful Congregations*.

Stanley, Andy. *The Principle of the Path*.

3DM: *3DM is a group of everyday people around the world who follow Jesus together, multiply disciples who make disciples, and empower spiritual families to live on mission for the sake of the lost.*

Warren, Rick. *The Purpose Driven Church: Growth Without Compromising Your Message & Mission.*

Welch, Robert H. *Church Administration.*

Bible Versions Cited:

Amplified (amp)

Easy to Read (erv)

Holman Bible (hcsb)

King James (kjv)

The Living Bible (tlb)

The Message (msg)

The Voice (voice)

Made in the USA
Middletown, DE
07 February 2025